Functional Vocabulary
for Adolescents & Adults

Beverly Plass

Skill Area: Vocabulary
Ages: 12-22
Grades: 7 and up

LinguiSystems

LinguiSystems, Inc.
3100 4th Avenue
East Moline, IL 61244-9700
800-776-4332
FAX: 800-577-4555
E-mail: service@linguisystems.com
Web: linguisystems.com

Copyright © 2005 LinguiSystems, Inc.

All of our products are copyrighted to protect the fine work of our authors. You may only copy the pictures as needed for your own use with students or clients. Any other reproduction or distribution of the pages in this book is prohibited, including copy book to use as another p or "master" copy.

The enclosed CD is for use and convenience. It copy this CD or store its multi-user network.

Printed in the U.S.A.

ISBN 0-7606-0629-3

About the Author

Beverly Plass, M.A., CCC-SLP, is a speech-language pathologist in the Irvine Unified School District in Irvine, California, and in private practice. She has worked with adolescents with developmental disabilities for the past 14 years. She has found that the key to student success is tied to their ability to understand and communicate about living, working, and playing.

Functional Vocabulary for Adolescents and Adults is Bev's fourth publication with LinguiSystems. She is also the author of *SPARC-R & S, SPARC-Artic Junior,* and *SPARC-L*.

Dedication

Thanks to my students for sharing their love for life

Acknowledgments

I'd like to thank three outstanding teachers: Carol Constantin, Carlon Fagan, and Liz Krogsdale for modeling creative and productive ways to teach functional curriculum to young adults with developmental disabilities. I am fortunate to have collaborated with them over the past 14 years. I am grateful to them for what I have learned and how it significantly influenced the development of this book.

Table of Contents

Introduction 6

Vocabulary at Home

Bathroom 8
Bedroom 10
Clothing 12
Clothing for Men 14
Clothing for Winter 16
Clothing for Women 18
Grooming – Hair Care 20
Grooming – Teeth & Fingernails 22
Grooming – Washing & Shaving 24
Kitchen – Appliances 26
Kitchen – Cooking 28
Kitchen – Cookware/Bakeware 30
Kitchen – Cutting Utensils 32
Kitchen – Tableware 34
Kitchen – Utensils 1 36
Kitchen – Utensils 2 38
Kitchen – Washing Dishes 40
Laundry – Nouns 42
Laundry – Verbs 44
Nutrition – Breads & Grains 46
Nutrition – Fruits 48
Nutrition – Meat & Protein 50
Nutrition – Milk, Yogurt, & Cheese 52
Nutrition – Vegetables 54
What's for Breakfast? 56
What's for Dinner? 58
What's for Lunch? 60

Vocabulary in the Community

Apartment 62
ATM (Automated Teller Machine) 64
Bank 66
City Bus 68
Clothing Store 70
Dentist's Office 72
Discount Department Store 74
Doctor's Office 76
Fast-Food Restaurant 78
Grocery Shopping 80
Grocery Store 82
Hardware Store 84
Library/Bookstore 86
Pet Store 88
Restaurant 90
School Supplies 92
Signs 94
Sporting Goods Store 96
Stationery Store 98
Toy Store 100

Vocabulary at Work

Job Choices 102
Getting a Job 104
What to Wear to Work 106
People You Work With 108
Attributes 110
Baker Helper 112
Dining Room Attendant – Fast-Food Restaurant 114

Dining Room Attendant – Restaurant	116
Floor Cleaning Supplies	118
Housecleaning Supplies	120
Laundry Worker	122
Lawn and Garden Tools	124
Office Helper Tasks	126
Office Helper Advanced Tasks	128
Stock Clerk	130
Stock Clerk – Clothing Store	132
Stock Clerk Tasks	134
Vehicle Cleaning Supplies	136

Vocabulary During Leisure Activities

Amusement Park	138
Arcade	140
Art	142
Baseball	144
Basketball	146
Birthday Party	148
Board Games	150
Bowling	152
Camping	154
Carnival	156
Crafts	158
Dance	160
Electronic Entertainment	162
Football	164
Fun Choices	166
Gym	168
Horseback Riding	170
Miniature Golf	172
Movie Theater	174
Poker	176
Soccer	178

Introduction

I once had two students who did job training at a nursery. They filled pots with soil and planted cuttings into each pot. Thirty-six pots were arranged in a flat. One student worked steadily and completed 10-12 flats in a two hour period. He was a quiet guy. He would respond with one- to two-word utterances if prodded, but he preferred to stick to his work. The young lady, however, was overly friendly. Each day, she greeted the co-workers with a loud, "I'm so glad to see you! What have you been up to?" She often stopped working to chat with the other workers. At the end of the two-hour period, she typically completed one to two flats.

At the end of the year, the nursery owners offered employment to one of the workers, which was the ultimate goal of our job training program. We assumed the job would go to the hardworking, productive young man. Instead, the owners chose the young lady because they felt that they could talk to her.

I later read studies supporting the idea that employees who can communicate effectively at work are more successful at keeping their jobs. That is why I feel it is imperative to teach functional vocabulary to teens and young adults with developmental disabilities.

Functional Vocabulary for Adolescents & Adults helps speech-language pathologists and special education teachers teach clients to understand and communicate about daily living. You can teach vocabulary related to the home, the community, work, and leisure activities. The lessons are geared toward clients with developmental disabilities, autism, and/or English as a Second Language. The flexible format allows you to cater the lessons to a wide range of ability levels.

Receptive tasks are appropriate for your clients who are non-verbal or new to learning English. These activities allow the client to hear the target vocabulary words several times, respond by pointing, and apply the knowledge to real situations. The receptive tasks also include a "visual memory" component, which helps clients learn to communicate about things not present.

Expressive tasks begin with simple picture-naming, sentence imitation, and sentence completion. This allows clients with autism and clients beginning to use short utterances to use the vocabulary in simple sentences. The expressive tasks then expand to identifying categories, explaining functions, sequencing events, and recalling information. The recalling tasks are to help clients visualize and discuss things not present. Expressive activities allow clients to use the vocabulary during meaningful and functional activities. At the highest level, critical thinking and problem solving questions allow the client to use the new vocabulary while thinking of solutions to real-life predicaments.

You do not need to follow the units in this book sequentially. You can collaborate and choose lessons that correspond with classroom units. For example, if the class is going to the grocery store, you can use the units about nutrition, mealtimes, grocery shopping, and the grocery store. If your clients are visiting job sites, you can use the units that correspond to the occupations they'll be observing and the places in the community they'll be visiting. Note: In the **Vocabulary at Work** section, I used the *Dictionary of Occupational Titles* (United States Department of Labor – Fourth Edition, Revised 1991, which is available online at www.oalj.dol.gov/libdot.htm) as a reference when determining how to label the job titles that are featured in this book. Feel free to modify the terminology so that it fits your program or the job titles available in your area.

For any unit, you do not need to ask all of the questions in each section. One client may focus on understanding the vocabulary while another client practices using the vocabulary in various sentences and answers questions. A third client can target problem solving tasks using the same topic. You can also modify the expectations for any task. For example, in the *Expressive Vocabulary* section of a unit, you may ask one client to recall all six pictures and another client to recall only three pictures. The flexibility allows you the freedom to meet the individual language needs of your clients across all of the topic areas.

You may also use the pictures in this book for other activities:

- Create written language assignments that correspond with the vocabulary. Clients can write definitions and answer the expressive questions in writing.

- Copy the pictures onto card stock. Cut them out and laminate them to use for picture communication books.

- Have clients create personal dictionaries by adding a picture page to their folders each time they learn new words.

- Use the community pictures to have clients help plan the next Community-Based Instruction.

- Use the vocational pictures as a job interest survey.

- Use the pictures during a scavenger hunt while on Community-Based Instruction.

- Have clients practice expanding utterances, using clear articulation, using appropriate voice levels, and speaking fluently.

Functional Vocabulary for Adolescents & Adults helps you teach your clients the terms they need to be successful in everyday life.

Beverly Plass

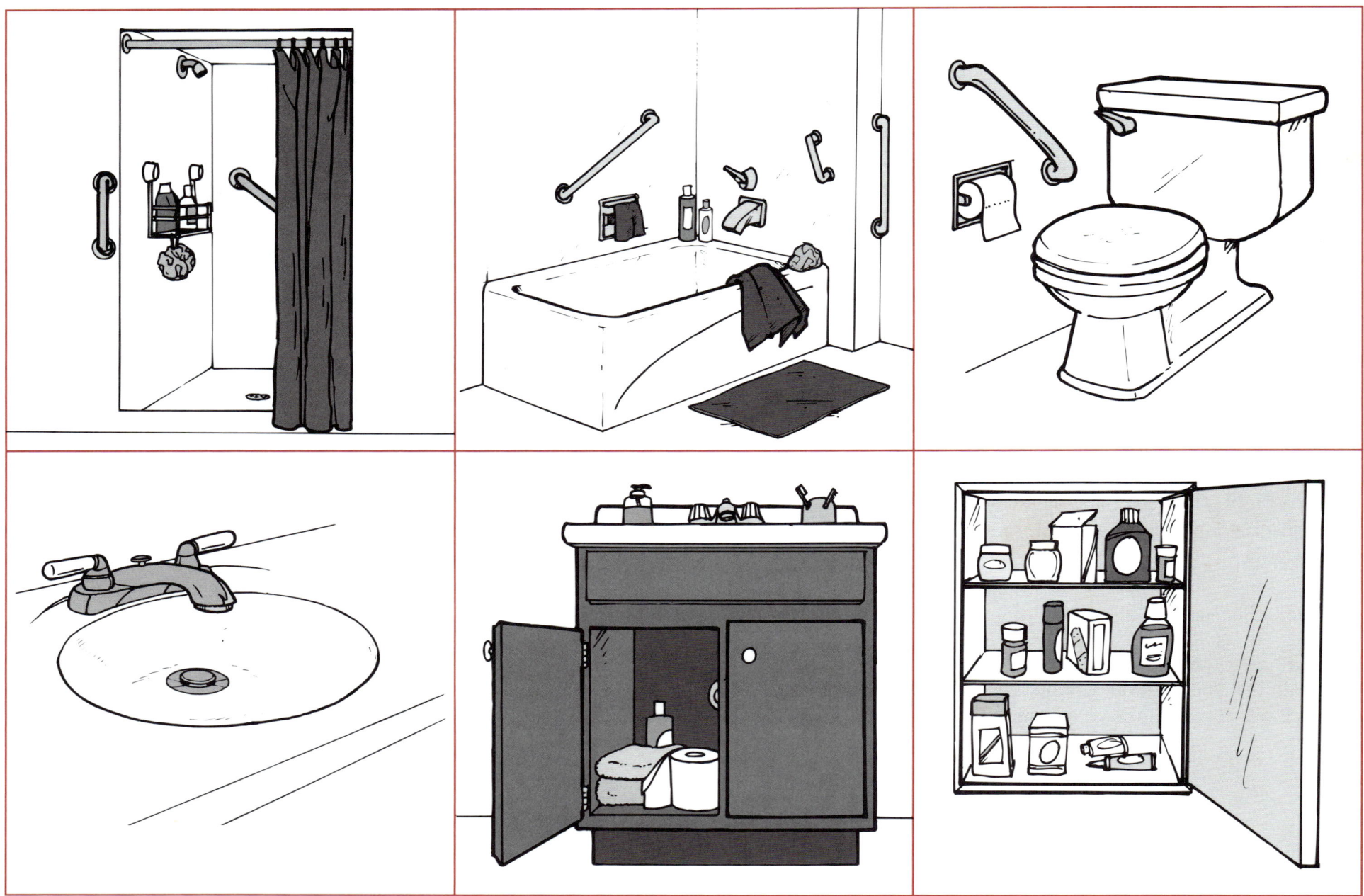

Bathroom

Receptive Vocabulary
Name each picture the client points to.

1. Point to the shower (medicine cabinet, toilet, sink, bathtub, vanity).
2. Show me where you can take a bath.
3. Where can you stand and clean your body?
4. Which flushes?
5. Where do you keep a toothbrush? shampoo?
6. Where do you keep medicine? a brush?
7. Where do you brush your teeth?
8. Where do you wash your hands?
9. Which do you like to take, a bath or a shower?
10. Which do you have in your bathroom?

Receptive Activities
Before doing these activities, make two copies of the picture grid. Cut apart one grid to make picture cards.

1. Give the student the picture grid. Have her match the picture cards to the pictures on the grid. *Where is the _____?*
2. Place the picture cards faceup on the table. Photocopy and cut out the picture cards from the Grooming: Hair Care and Teeth & Fingernails units. Have the student tell where she keeps each item. *Show me where you keep _____.*
3. Place the picture cards faceup on the table. Have the student follow your directions. *Touch the _____. Take the _____. Hand me the _____. Point to the _____. Turn over the _____.*
4. Cover three to six of the pictures on the picture grid. Show the student a picture card and have her tell you where it was on the picture grid. *Where was the _____?*
5. Use ads from a hardware store or look on a home remodeling website. *Find a _____.*
6. Visit a hardware store, an apartment, or a student's home. Have the student find items that match the pictures. *Let's look for a _____.*

Word/Sentence Imitation and Sentence Completion
1. Ask the client to repeat each word after you say it. *Say _____.*
2. Use each word to complete the sentence *This is a _____.* Have the client repeat your sentences.
3. Print *A _____ is in the bathroom* on a card. Have the client complete the sentence using the vocabulary words.

Expressive Vocabulary
1. Name each picture.
2. What do all of these have in common?
3. After shopping, where would you put shampoo (toothpaste, bar of soap, toilet paper, aspirin)?
4. While putting away clean laundry, where would you put towels (washcloths, the bath mat)?
5. What do you do in the bathtub? shower?
6. What do you do at the sink?
7. Name three things you keep in your medicine cabinet.
8. Tell three things you keep in your vanity.
9. What does your bathroom look like?
10. (Cover the pictures.) Name six items in your bathroom.

Expressive Activity
Find websites that include bathroom accessories, such as bath mats, shower curtains, washcloths, and soap dishes, or look in bathroom supply store ads. Talk with the client about where she could put each item in her bathroom.

Critical Thinking and Problem Solving
1. What would you do if the bath water was too hot?
2. What would you do if the bathroom floor got wet?
3. What could you do if the sink was clogged?
4. What do you do to keep your body clean?
5. Where should you keep medicine so that small children can't reach it?
6. If the bathroom door is closed, how can you find out if someone is inside?
7. Why do we close the bathroom door when using the toilet?
8. Why is it a good idea to shower or bathe daily?
9. How do you know if you need to shower or bathe?
10. How does keeping your body clean make a good impression?

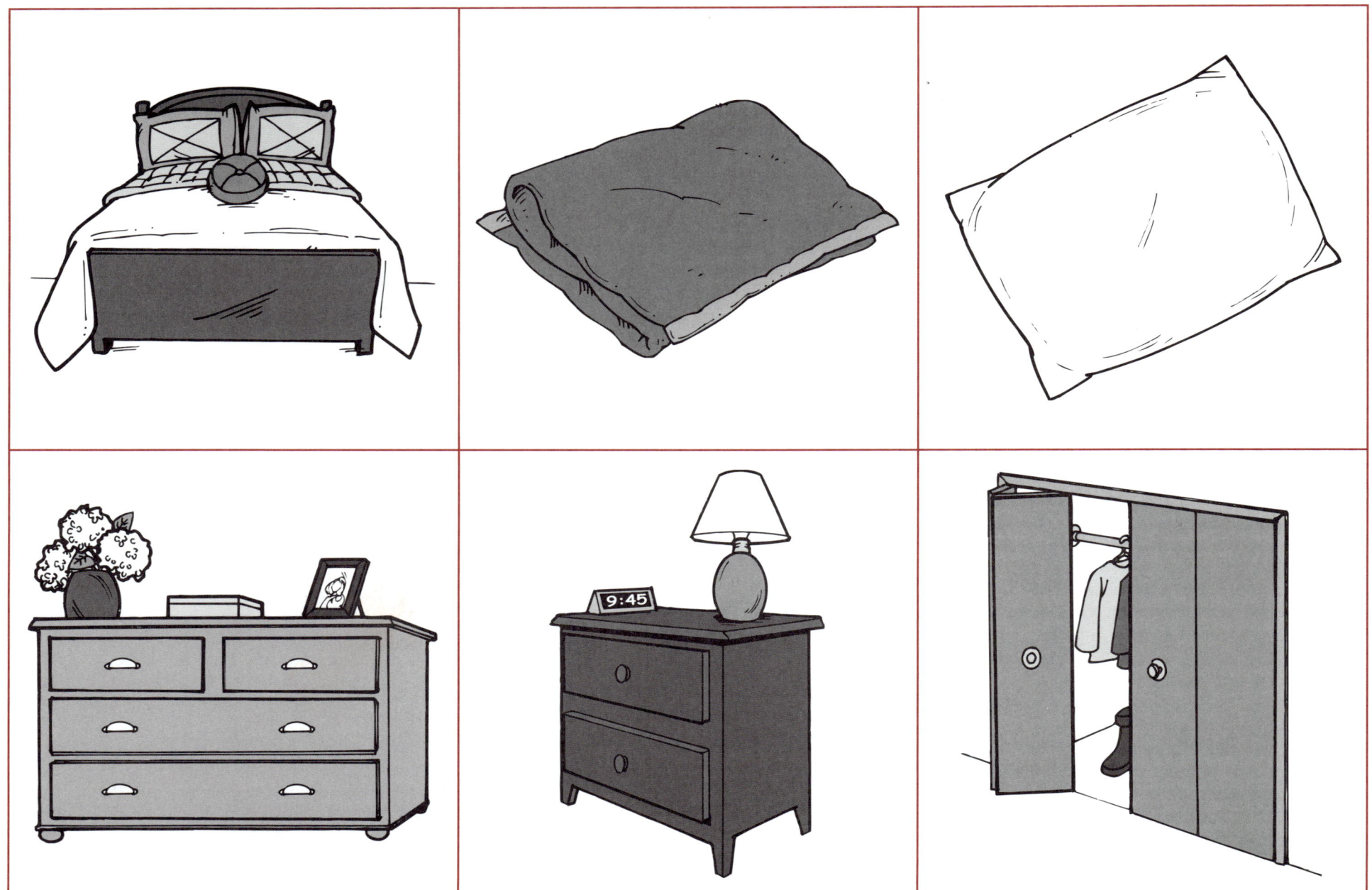

Bedroom

Receptive Vocabulary
Name each picture the client points to.

1. Point to the pillow (bed, nightstand, blanket, dresser, closet).
2. Show me where you sleep.
3. Which do you put your head on?
4. Which keeps you warm at night?
5. Where do you keep your pants? shirts?
6. Where do you keep your shoes? socks?
7. Which have drawers?
8. Which has doors?
9. Which are soft?
10. Show me what you have in your room.

Receptive Activities
Before doing these activities, make two copies of the picture grid. Cut apart one grid to make picture cards.

1. Give the client the picture grid. Have him match the picture cards to the pictures on the grid. *Where is the _____?*
2. Play a game of Bingo. Use pennies as markers.
3. Cut out pictures of items in a bedroom from magazines or catalogs. Glue them to a sheet of paper, creating a few bedrooms. *Show me the _____.*
4. Place the picture cards faceup on the table. Have the client follow your directions. *Touch the _____. Take the _____. Hand me the _____. Point to the _____. Turn over the _____.*
5. Cover three to six pictures on the picture grid. Show the client a picture card and have him tell you where it was on the picture grid. *Where was the _____?*
6. Use ads from a department store or bedroom furniture store, or a website that contains bedroom furniture. *Find a _____.*
7. Visit a furniture store, a department store, or an apartment. Find items that match the pictures. *Let's look for a _____.*

Word/Sentence Imitation and Sentence Completion
1. Ask the client to repeat each word after you say it. *Say _____.*
2. Use each word to complete the sentence *Here is a _____.* Have the client repeat your sentences.
3. Print *A _____ is in the bedroom* on a card. Have the client complete the sentence using the vocabulary words.

Expressive Vocabulary
1. Name each picture.
2. What do all of these items have in common?
3. What does your bed look like?
4. What does the furniture in your bedroom look like?
5. When putting away clean clothes, where would you put _____ (pajamas, shirts, pants, socks, shoes, jacket, shorts)?
6. Name three things you keep in your closet.
7. Tell three things you keep in your dresser.
8. How are a dresser and a closet different?
9. What do you do to keep your room clean?
10. (Cover the pictures.) Name six items in your bedroom.

Expressive Activity
Use newspaper ads or websites that contain bedroom furniture and furnishings. Let the client cut out pictures and arrange them on paper to design a bedroom. Have the client discuss why he chose particular items and where he would put them in the room and why.

Critical Thinking and Problem Solving
1. What could you do if you were cold at night while sleeping?
2. What would you do if you overslept?
3. What would you do if there were no socks in your drawer?
4. When changing clothes, what do you do with your dirty clothes?
5. What do you do to keep your room clean?
6. What could you do if your closet and dresser are full and you got some new clothes?
7. What could you do to give you more time to get ready in the morning?
8. What could you do if you aren't getting enough sleep at night?
9. How do you wake up in the morning?
10. How could you plan what you are going to wear each day?

Clothing

Receptive Vocabulary
Name each picture the client points to.

1. Point to the shorts (pajamas, pants, belt, socks, and shirt).
2. Show me what goes on your feet.
3. Which goes on your legs?
4. Which holds up your pants?
5. Which do you wear when you sleep?
6. Which could you wear to school?
7. Which could you wear to work?
8. Which would you wear if it was hot?
9. Which of these do you have at home?
10. Look at what you are wearing today. Point to your _____.

Receptive Activities
Before doing these activities, make two copies of the picture grid. Cut apart one grid to make picture cards.

1. Give the client the picture grid. Have her match the picture cards to the pictures on the grid. *Where is/are the _____?*
2. Cut out pictures of clothing from magazines or catalogs. Glue them to a sheet of paper, creating a few outfits. *Show me the _____.*
3. Bring in a laundry basket full of clean clothes. Have the client practice sorting and folding the clothes. *Put the _____ in this pile. Fold the _____.*
4. Place the picture cards faceup on the table. Have the client follow your directions. *Touch the _____. Take the _____. Hand me the _____. Point to the _____. Turn over the _____.*
5. Cover three to six pictures on the picture grid. Show the client a picture card and have her tell you where it was on the picture grid. *Where was/were the _____?*
6. Use ads, catalogs, or websites that contain clothing. *Find (a) _____.*
7. Visit a clothing store or a department store. Use the pictures as a shopping list. *Let's look for (a) _____.*

Word/Sentence Imitation and Sentence Completion
1. Ask the client to repeat each word after you say it. *Say _____.*
2. Use each word to complete the sentence *I wear (a) _____.* Have the client repeat your sentences.
3. Print *I have (a) _____* on a card. Have the client complete the sentence using the vocabulary words.

Expressive Vocabulary
1. Name each picture.
2. What do all of these items have in common?
3. Describe what you are wearing.
4. Where do you keep your clothes?
5. Where can you buy clothing?
6. What kinds of shirts are there?
7. What kinds of pants are there?
8. When would you wear shorts?
9. Why do people wear belts?
10. (Cover the pictures.) Name six clothing items.

Expressive Activity
Have two clients pretend to put on a fashion show. One client can model the clothes she is wearing while the other describes the outfit. Encourage the MC to "ham it up" and make the outfit sound glamorous.

Critical Thinking and Problem Solving
1. What can you do about wrinkled clothes?
2. What do you do if a button falls off?
3. What clothes are appropriate to wear to school?
4. What would you wear to a job interview?
5. What clothes would you pack for a weekend vacation?
6. How do the clothes you wear help make an impression?
7. How does the weather affect what you plan to wear?
8. While buying clothes, how can you tell if the clothes fit?
9. How can you tell if your clothes are dirty?
10. How can you clean clothes that are dirty?

Vocabulary at Home: Clothing for Men

Clothing for Men

Receptive Vocabulary
Name each picture the client points to.

1. Point to the dress shirt (T-shirt, polo shirt, underwear, tie, suit).
2. Show me which you could wear to school.
3. Which could you wear to a wedding?
4. Which do you have at home?
5. Which are you wearing today?
6. Which go on a hanger?
7. Which can you fold and put in a drawer?
8. Which would you wear with the suit?
9. Which could you wear with shorts?
10. Which is personal?

Receptive Activities
Before doing these activities, make two copies of the picture grid. Cut apart one grid to make picture cards.

1. Give the client the picture grid. Have him match the picture cards to the pictures on the grid. *Where is/are the _____?*
2. Cut out pictures of men's clothing from magazines or catalogs. Glue them to a sheet of paper, creating a few outfits. *Show me the _____.*
3. Bring in men's T-shirts, polo shirts, and hangers. *Pretend you work at a clothing store. Fold the T-shirts. Hang the polo shirts.*
4. Place the picture cards faceup on the table. Have the client follow your directions. *Touch the _____. Take the _____. Hand me the _____. Point to the _____. Turn over the _____.*
5. Cover three to six pictures on the picture grid. Show the client a picture card and have him tell you where it was on the picture grid. *Where was/were the _____?*
6. Use ads, catalogs, or websites that contain men's clothing. *Find (a) _____.*
7. Visit a clothing store or a department store. Use the pictures as a shopping list. *Let's look for (a) _____.*

Word/Sentence Imitation and Sentence Completion
1. Ask the client to repeat each word after you say it. *Say _____.*
2. Use each word to complete the sentence *I can wear (a) _____.* Have the client repeat your sentences.
3. Print *I want to buy (a) _____* on a card. Have the client complete the sentence using the vocabulary words.

Expressive Vocabulary
1. Name each picture.
2. What do all of these items have in common?
3. Which do you have?
4. Describe what you are wearing.
5. What would you wear to a formal dance?
6. What would you wear to a job interview?
7. What would you wear to exercise?
8. Where could you buy T-shirts?
9. Describe different kinds of shirts.
10. (Cover the pictures.) Name six men's clothing items.

Expressive Activity
Have the client pretend to shop for new clothes. He can look at clothing ads or catalogs, or on the Internet. Ask the client to talk about the clothes he likes and dislikes.

Critical Thinking and Problem Solving
1. What could you do if you didn't know how to tie a tie?
2. What could you do if you got a spot on your shirt?
3. What if a button is loose on your clothing?
4. What if your pants are wrinkled?
5. When changing in a dressing room, why should you close the door?
6. Why shouldn't others see you in your underwear?
7. Tell how your clothing helps make an impression on others.
8. When shopping, how can you tell if a dress shirt fits you?
9. How do you know what size T-shirt or underwear to buy?
10. How should you act when wearing a suit?

Vocabulary at Home: Clothing for Winter

Clothing for Winter

Receptive Vocabulary
Name each picture the client points to.

1. Point to the sweater (scarf, coat, gloves, stocking cap, boots).
2. Show me which keeps your hands warm.
3. Which keeps your feet dry and warm?
4. Which keeps your head warm?
5. Which keeps your neck warm?
6. Which keep your chest and arms warm?
7. Which would you wear in the snow?
8. Which would you wear in the rain?
9. Which would you keep in the closet?
10. Which are soft?

Receptive Activities
Before doing these activities, make two copies of the picture grid. Cut apart one grid to make picture cards.

1. Give the client the picture grid. Have him match the picture cards to the pictures on the grid. *Where is/are the _____?*
2. Cut out pictures of winter clothing from magazines or catalogs. Glue them to a sheet of paper. *Show me the _____.*
3. Play a pantomime game using the picture cards or real items. *Show me how you put this on.*
4. Place the picture cards faceup on the table. Have the client follow your directions. *Touch the _____. Take the _____. Hand me the _____. Point to the _____. Turn over the _____.*
5. Cover three to six pictures on the picture grid. Show the client a picture card and have him tell you where it was on the picture grid. *Where was/were the _____?*
6. Use ads, catalogs, or websites that contain winter clothing. *Find (a) _____.*
7. Visit a department store or a sporting goods store. Use the pictures as a shopping list. *Let's look for (a) _____.*

Word/Sentence Imitation and Sentence Completion
1. Ask the client to repeat each word after you say it. *Say _____.*
2. Use each word to complete the sentence *I have a warm (pair of) _____.* Have the client repeat your sentences.
3. Print *I can wear (a) _____* on a card. Have the client complete the sentence using the vocabulary words.

Expressive Vocabulary
1. Name each picture.
2. What do all of these items have in common?
3. Which do you have at home?
4. What does your winter coat look like?
5. Why would you wear boots?
6. Why would you wear gloves?
7. How are gloves and mittens different?
8. Describe different kinds of winter coats.
9. Describe how you would shop for winter clothes.
10. (Cover the pictures.) Name six clothing items worn in the winter.

Expressive Activity
Have the client pretend to shop for new winter clothes. He can look at clothing ads or catalogs, or on the Internet. Ask the client to talk about the clothes he likes and dislikes.

Critical Thinking and Problem Solving
1. If the meteorologist predicts rain, what would you wear?
2. If the meteorologist predicts snow, what would you wear?
3. If the meteorologist predicts sunshine, what would you wear?
4. If the meteorologist predicts wind, what would you wear?
5. Why do some people have more than one coat?
6. Why do you sometimes wear a sweater in the summertime?
7. Why is it important to wear a hat when it is cold outside?
8. How do you know what the weather is outside?
9. How do you know what the weather will be later?
10. How does the weather affect what you wear?

Vocabulary at Home: Clothing for Women
Functional Vocabulary for Adolescents & Adults

Clothing for Women

Receptive Vocabulary
Name each picture the client points to.

1. Point to the bra (slip, blouse, dress, underwear, skirt).
2. Show me which can hang on a hanger.
3. Which go in a dresser?
4. Which are private?
5. Which go with the blouse?
6. Which go with the bra?
7. Which go under a dress?
8. Show me which you have.
9. Which would a woman wear to a job interview?
10. Which would a woman wear to a wedding?

Receptive Activities
Before doing these activities, make two copies of the picture grid. Cut apart one grid to make picture cards.

1. Give the client the picture grid. Have her match the picture cards to the pictures on the grid. *Where is the _____?*
2. Cut out pictures of women's clothing from magazines or catalogs. Glue them to a sheet of paper, creating a few outfits. *Show me the _____.*
3. Bring in dresses, blouses, skirts, and hangers. *Pretend you work at a clothing store. Put the skirts together. Hang up the dresses. Fold the blouses.*
4. Place the picture cards faceup on the table. Have the client follow your directions. *Touch the _____. Take the _____. Hand me the _____. Point to the _____. Turn over the _____.*
5. Cover three to six pictures on the picture grid. Show the client a picture card and have her tell you where it was on the picture grid. *Where was the _____?*
6. Use ads, catalogs, or websites that contain women's clothing. *Find (a) _____.*
7. Visit a clothing store or a department store. Use the pictures as a shopping list. *Let's look for (a) _____.*

Word/Sentence Imitation and Sentence Completion
1. Ask the client to repeat each word after you say it. *Say _____.*
2. Use each word to complete the sentence *I wear (a) _____.* Have the client repeat your sentences.
3. Print *I bought (a) _____* on a card. Have the client complete the sentence using the vocabulary words.

Expressive Vocabulary
1. Name each picture.
2. Which do you have at home?
3. Which are personal?
4. Where could a woman wear a dress?
5. Where could a woman wear a skirt and blouse?
6. Where could a woman buy a dress?
7. Where can women buy bras and underwear?
8. How are dresses and skirts different?
9. Tell how you keep your clothes clean.
10. (Cover the pictures.) Name six women's clothing items.

Expressive Activity
Have the client pretend to shop for new clothes. She can look at clothing ads or catalogs, or on the Internet. Ask the client to talk about the clothes she likes and dislikes.

Critical Thinking and Problem Solving
1. What could you do if your dress got a spot on it?
2. What could you do if a button on your blouse is loose?
3. What could you do if your bra unhooks?
4. What could you do if your skirt is wrinkled?
5. When changing in a dressing room, why should you close the door?
6. Why shouldn't others see you in your underwear?
7. How can you tell if your slip is showing?
8. When shopping, how can you tell if a dress fits you?
9. How do you know what size bra or underwear to buy?
10. How should you sit if you are wearing a dress or skirt?

Vocabulary at Home: Grooming – Hair Care
Functional Vocabulary for Adolescents & Adults

Grooming – Hair Care

Receptive Vocabulary
Name each picture the client points to.

1. Point to the mirror (brush, conditioner, blow dryer, comb, shampoo).
2. Show me what you use to brush your hair.
3. Which do you use to comb your hair?
4. Which do you use to clean your hair?
5. Which makes your hair soft?
6. Which one is used for drying hair?
7. Which could you use to see your face?
8. Which do you use in the shower or bathtub?
9. Which come in bottles?
10. Which do you have at your home?

Receptive Activities
Before doing these activities, make two copies of the picture grid. Cut apart one grid to make picture cards.

1. Give the client the picture grid. Have her match the picture cards to the pictures on the grid. *Where is the _____?*
2. Place a real bottle of shampoo, brush, comb, etc. on the table. Give a picture card to the client and have her put it by the matching item. *Find the _____.*
3. Play a pantomime game using the picture cards or real items. *Show me how you use this.*
4. Place the picture cards faceup on the table. Have the client follow your directions. *Touch the _____. Take the _____. Hand me the _____. Point to the _____. Turn over the _____.*
5. Cover three to six pictures on the picture grid. Show the client a picture card and have her tell you where it was on the picture grid. *Where was the _____?*
6. Use ads from a drug store or grocery store. *Find (a) _____.*
7. Visit a drug store or a grocery store. Use the pictures as a shopping list. *Let's look for (a) _____.*

Word/Sentence Imitation and Sentence Completion
1. Ask the client to repeat each word after you say it. *Say _____.*
2. Use each word to complete the sentence *I see (a) _____.* Have the client repeat your sentences.
3. Print *I use (a) _____* on a card. Have the client complete the sentence using the vocabulary words.

Expressive Vocabulary
1. Name each picture.
2. What do all of these items have in common?
3. When do you wash your hair?
4. Where do you keep these items?
5. What brand/color of _____ do you use?
6. What do you do with (a) _____?
7. Where do you buy these items?
8. Which have you used today?
9. Describe how you wash and fix your hair.
10. (Cover the pictures.) Name five items that you use on your hair.

Expressive Activity
Have the client pretend she's going on a trip. Ask her to make a list of the hair care items she would need to pack.

Critical Thinking and Problem Solving
1. What do you do if your hair is dirty?
2. What do you do to have clean and neat hair?
3. What can you do if your hair is messy?
4. What do you do if you need a hair cut?
5. What should you do if you use up all of the shampoo?
6. What could you get better at when caring for your hair?
7. How do you know if your hair is messy?
8. How do you know if you need a hair cut?
9. How do you know if your hair is dirty?
10. How does clean and neat hair help make a good impression?

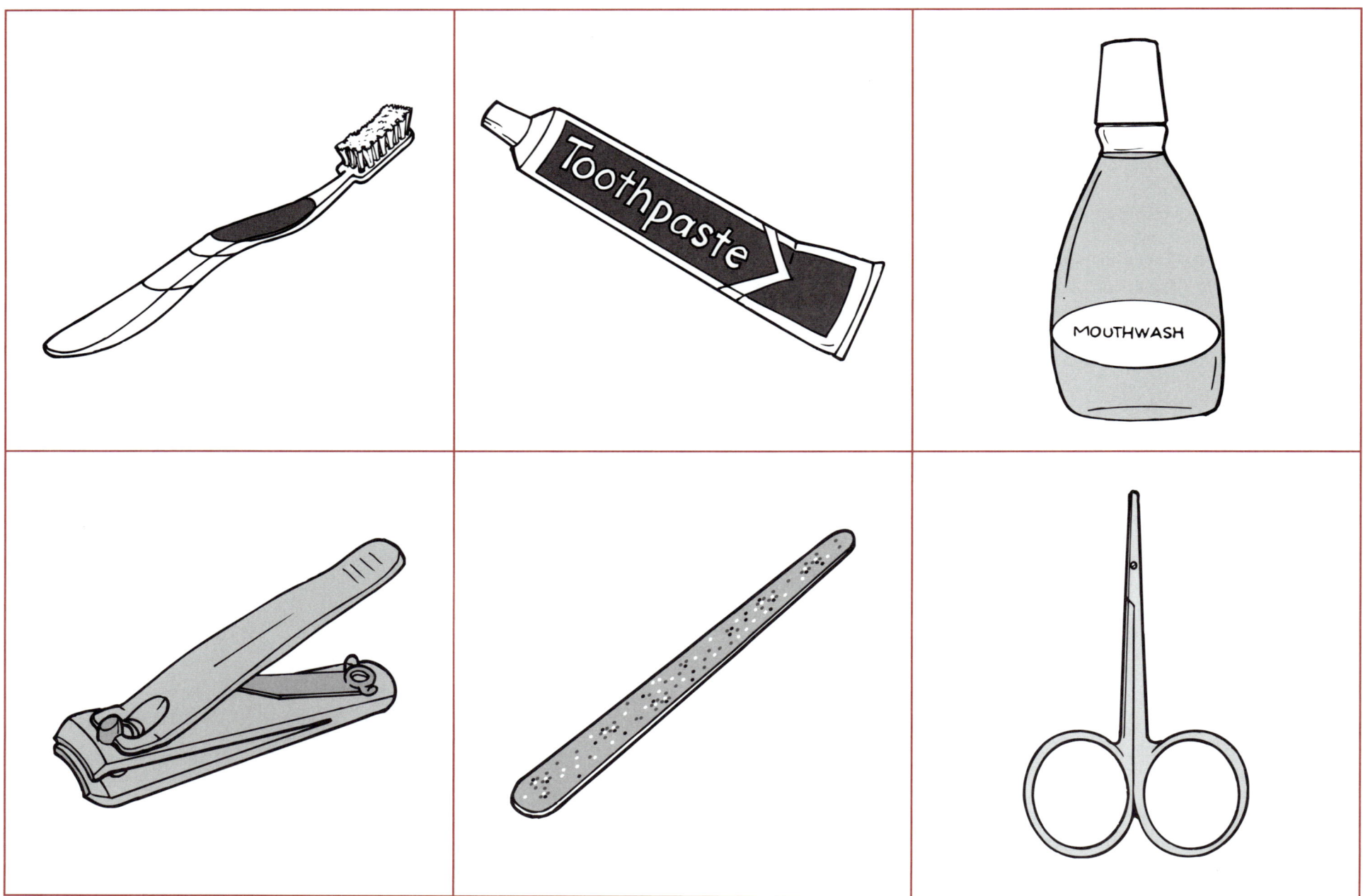

Vocabulary at Home: Grooming – Teeth & Fingernails
Functional Vocabulary for Adolescents & Adults

Grooming – Teeth & Fingernails

Receptive Vocabulary
Name each picture the client points to.

1. Point to the toothbrush (emery board, nail scissors, toothpaste, mouthwash, nail clippers).
2. Show me which one goes on your toothbrush.
3. Which do you use to brush your teeth?
4. Which is used for rinsing out your mouth?
5. Which do you use to cut your fingernails?
6. Which is used to file fingernails?
7. Which clean your teeth and mouth?
8. Which keep your fingernails trimmed and shaped nicely?
9. Which do you have at home?
10. Which do you use?

Receptive Activities
Before doing these activities, make two copies of the picture grid. Cut apart one grid to make picture cards.

1. Give the client the picture grid. Have him match the picture cards to the pictures on the grid. *Where is/are the _____?*
2. Place a real toothbrush, tube of toothpaste, bottle of mouthwash, etc. on the table. Give a picture card to the client and have him put it by the matching item. *Find the _____.*
3. Play a pantomime game using the picture cards or real items. *Show me how you use this.*
4. Place the picture cards faceup on the table. Have the client follow your directions. *Touch the _____. Take the _____. Hand me the _____. Point to the _____. Turn over the _____.*
5. Cover three to six pictures on the picture grid. Show the client a picture card and have him tell you where it was on the picture grid. *Where was/were the _____?*
6. Use ads from a drug store or grocery store. *Find (a/an) _____.*
7. Visit a drug store or a grocery store. Use the pictures as a shopping list. *Let's look for (a/an) _____.*

Word/Sentence Imitation and Sentence Completion
1. Ask the client to repeat each word after you say it. *Say _____.*
2. Use each word to complete the sentence *I have (a/an) _____.* Have the client repeat your sentences.
3. Print *Get the _____* on a card. Have the client complete the sentence using the vocabulary words.

Expressive Vocabulary
1. Name each picture.
2. What do you do with (a/an) _____?
3. Which of these do you use? when?
4. What brand/color of _____ do you use?
5. Where do you keep these items?
6. What do toothpaste, a toothbrush, and mouthwash have in common?
7. What do nail clippers, an emery board, and scissors have in common?
8. Describe how you clean your teeth.
9. Tell how you trim your nails.
10. (Cover the pictures.) Name six grooming items.

Expressive Activity
Have clients bring in their own toothbrushes and nail clippers. Ask them to brush their teeth, use mouthwash, and trim their nails. Have them describe how they do each step.

Critical Thinking and Problem Solving
1. If you were packing for a trip, what would you put in your toiletries bag?
2. What do you do if your nails are dirty?
3. What could happen if you pick your fingernails?
4. Why should we brush our teeth every day?
5. What do you do to keep your teeth clean?
6. What do you do to keep your nails neat and trim?
7. How do you know if your fingernails need to be trimmed?
8. How can you prevent bad breath?
9. How do clean teeth help make a good impression?
10. How do neat fingernails help make a good impression?

Grooming – Washing & Shaving

Receptive Vocabulary
Name each picture the client points to.

1. Point to the washcloth (razor, soap, deodorant, towel, shaving cream).
2. Show me what helps you get your hands clean.
3. Which one is used for shaving?
4. Before shaving, what does a man smear on his chin?
5. Which do you dry off with?
6. Which goes on your underarms?
7. Which do you use to wash your face?
8. Which do you have at home?
9. Which have a smell?
10. Which did you use today?

Receptive Activities
Before doing these activities, make two copies of the picture grid. Cut apart one grid to make picture cards.

1. Give the client the picture grid. Have him match the picture cards to the pictures on the grid. *Where is the _____?*
2. Place a real washcloth, bar of soap, etc. on the table. Give a picture card to the client and have him put it by the matching item. *Find the _____.*
3. Play a pantomime game using the picture cards or real items. *Show me how you use this.* (If using real items, make sure the razor has on a safety guard.)
4. Place the picture cards faceup on the table. Have the client follow your directions. *Touch the _____. Take the _____. Hand me the _____. Point to the _____. Turn over the _____.*
5. Cover three to six pictures on the picture grid. Show the client a picture card and have him tell you where it was on the picture grid. *Where was the _____?*
6. Use ads from a drug store or a grocery store. *Find (a) _____.*
7. Visit a drug store or a grocery store. Use the pictures as a shopping list. *Let's look for (a) _____.*

Word/Sentence Imitation and Sentence Completion
1. Ask the client to repeat each word after you say it. *Say _____.*
2. Use each word to complete the sentence *I see (a) _____.* Have the client repeat your sentences.
3. Print *I use (a) _____* on a card. Have the client complete the sentence using the vocabulary words.

Expressive Vocabulary
1. Name each picture.
2. What do all of these items have in common?
3. Which do you have at home?
4. What brand/color of _____ do you use?
5. What do you do with (a) _____?
6. Which have you used today?
7. Describe how you wash your hands.
8. Describe how you shave.
9. Describe how you get ready in the morning.
10. (Cover the pictures.) Name six grooming items.

Expressive Activity
Have the client teach a friend how to wash hands, shave, and use deodorant. Ask the client to model and describe the actions before his friend takes a turn. (Have clients use their own deodorant and razors for this activity.)

Critical Thinking and Problem Solving
1. What do you do so your armpits won't smell?
2. What do you do if you run out of deodorant?
3. What do you do if your washcloth is dirty?
4. What do you do to have good grooming?
5. What could you get better at when grooming?
6. Where do you put your towel after bathing?
7. Why do you wash your hands before eating?
8. How do you know if you need to shave?
9. How do you know if you missed a spot shaving?
10. How does good grooming help make a good impression?

Vocabulary at Home: Kitchen – Appliances
Functional Vocabulary for Adolescents & Adults

Kitchen – Appliances

Receptive Vocabulary
Name each picture the client points to.

1. Point to the refrigerator (microwave, oven, coffee maker, toaster, stove).
2. Show me which keeps milk cold.
3. Which reheats leftovers quickly?
4. Which do you use to make toast?
5. Which do you use to make coffee?
6. Which do you bake muffins in?
7. Which do you cook a pot of macaroni on?
8. Which do you have at school?
9. Which can get hot?
10. Which are plugged in?

Receptive Activities
Before doing these activities, make two copies of the picture grid. Cut apart one grid to make picture cards.

1. Give the client the picture grid. Have her match the picture cards to the pictures on the squares. *Where is the _____?*
2. Visit a kitchen or a cafeteria. Put a piece of tape on a picture card and give it to the client. Have her place the card on the matching item as a label.
3. Prepare food using one or more of these kitchen appliances. Talk about how to turn on and use each appliance.
4. Place the picture cards faceup on the table. Have the client follow your directions. *Touch the _____. Take the _____. Hand me the _____. Point to the _____. Turn over the _____.*
5. Cover three to six pictures on the picture grid. Show the client a picture card and have her tell you where it was on the picture grid. *Where was the _____?*
6. Use ads from a hardware store or an appliance store, or look on a website that contains kitchen appliances. *Find a/an _____.*
7. Visit an appliance store or hardware store. Use the pictures as a shopping list. *Let's look for a/an _____.*

Word/Sentence Imitation and Sentence Completion
1. Ask the client to repeat each word after you say it. *Say _____.*
2. Use each word to complete the sentence *The _____ is in the kitchen.* Have the client repeat your sentences.
3. Print *I see a/an _____* on a card. Have the client complete the sentence using the vocabulary words.

Expressive Vocabulary
1. Name each picture.
2. Which do you have at home?
3. What do your kitchen appliances look like?
4. What does each appliance do?
5. What do all of these items have in common?
6. Name three things you keep in a refrigerator.
7. What is the difference between a microwave and a toaster?
8. What is the difference between an oven and a stove?
9. Describe how to microwave a slice of pizza.
10. (Cover the pictures.) Name six kitchen appliances.

Expressive Activity
Have the client look up her favorite recipe in a cookbook. Ask her to tell where in the kitchen she would find the ingredients she needs and which appliances she would use to prepare the meal.

Critical Thinking and Problem Solving
1. What would you do if there was a bad odor inside your refrigerator?
2. What would you do if a casserole spilled in the oven?
3. What would you do if water started boiling over on your stove?
4. What would you do if soup boiled over in the microwave?
5. What would you do if your bread wasn't toasted enough?
6. What could you eat if the electricity went out?
7. How can you tell if the coffee is done brewing?
8. How can you prevent food from splattering in the microwave?
9. How do you know how long to cook a food item?
10. How do you protect your hands when using the oven, stove, and microwave?

Kitchen – Cooking

Receptive Vocabulary
Name each picture the client points to.

1. Point to slice (bake, grate, boil, simmer, fry).
2. Show me what you can do with cheese.
3. Which do you do to heat a sauce?
4. Which do you do to heat a casserole?
5. Which can you do to cook chicken?
6. Which do you do with a knife?
7. Which do you do with a grater?
8. Which do you do with a saucepan?
9. Which do you do with a frying pan?
10. Which do you know how to do?

Receptive Activities
Before doing these activities, make two copies of the picture grid. Cut apart one grid to make picture cards.

1. Give the client the picture grid. Have him match the picture cards to the pictures on the grid. *Which is _____?*
2. Prepare a food item that requires you to do some of these actions. Ask the client to do some of these tasks.
3. Watch a cooking show. Have the client place a picture card on the matching picture on the grid each time the chef performs one of these actions.
4. Place the picture cards faceup on the table. Have the client follow your directions. *Touch _____. Take _____. Hand me _____. Point to _____. Turn over _____.*
5. Cover three to six pictures on the picture grid. Show the client a picture card and have him tell you where it was on the picture grid. *Where was _____?*
6. Look through a cookbook that has several pictures in it. *Find a food that is sliced (grated, boiled, simmered, baked, fried).*
7. Look at a restaurant menu that has several pictures in it. *Find a food that is sliced (grated, boiled, simmered, baked, fried).*

Word/Sentence Imitation and Sentence Completion
1. Ask the client to repeat each word after you say it. *Say _____.*
2. Use each word to complete the sentence *I _____ the food.* Have the client repeat your sentences.
3. Print *She is _____ the food.* Have the client complete the sentence using the vocabulary words.

Expressive Vocabulary
1. Tell what is happening in each picture.
2. What utensils do you need to do each action?
3. Which are done on the stove? in the oven?
4. Which is done on a cutting board?
5. Name three things you can slice.
6. Name three things you can boil.
7. Name three things you can bake.
8. What is the difference between boiling and simmering?
9. Describe how you cook spaghetti noodles and sauce.
10. (Cover the pictures.) Name six cooking words.

Expressive Activity
Have the client look up his favorite recipes in a cookbook. Ask him to discuss how each food item is prepared using the vocabulary words.

Critical Thinking and Problem Solving
1. If a salad recipe calls for 1 cup of sliced carrots, what do you do?
2. What are some safety rules to follow while slicing?
3. If a pizza recipe calls for 1 cup of grated cheese, what do you do?
4. What are some safety rules to follow while grating?
5. If the recipe says to bake for 30-35 minutes, what do you do?
6. What do you do if the oven smells like something is burning?
7. If the recipe says to boil water, what do you do?
8. If the spaghetti sauce is to simmer, what do you do?
9. If grease is splattering from the frying pan, what should you do?
10. How do you know if pizza is done cooking?

Kitchen – Cookware/Bakeware

Receptive Vocabulary
Name each picture the client points to.

1. Point to the saucepan (muffin pan, skillet, casserole dish, wok, cookie sheet).
2. Show me which is used to heat soup.
3. Which is used to fry fish?
4. Which is used to stir-fry vegetables?
5. Which is used to bake muffins?
6. Which is used to bake cookies?
7. Which is used to bake a tuna casserole?
8. Which do you have at school?
9. Which do you have at your home?
10. Which are rectangular? round?

Receptive Activities
Before doing these activities, make two copies of the picture grid. Cut apart one grid to make picture cards.

1. Give the client the picture grid. Have her match the picture cards to the pictures on the grid. *Where is the _____?*
2. Place a real skillet, wok, etc. on the table. Give a picture card to the client and have her put it by the matching item. *Find the _____.*
3. Prepare food using one or more of these cookware/bakeware items. Have the client gather the items that you ask for.
4. Place the picture cards faceup on the table. Have the client follow your directions. *Touch the _____. Take the _____. Hand me the _____. Point to the _____. Turn over the _____.*
5. Cover three to six pictures on the picture grid. Show the client a picture card and have her tell you where it was on the picture grid. *Where was the _____?*
6. Use ads from a local store or a website that contains kitchen items. *Find a _____.*
7. Visit a kitchen or a store that sells kitchen items. Use the pictures as a shopping list. *Let's look for a _____.*

Word/Sentence Imitation and Sentence Completion
1. Ask the client to repeat each word after you say it. *Say _____.*
2. Use each word to complete the sentence *This is a _____.* Have the client repeat your sentences.
3. Print *I cook with a _____* on a card. Have the client complete the sentence using the vocabulary words.

Expressive Vocabulary
1. Name each picture.
2. Which do you have at home?
3. Which are used for baking? cooking?
4. How do you use a _____?
5. How are a saucepan and a wok different?
6. How are a casserole dish and a cookie sheet different?
7. Name three foods you can cook in a skillet.
8. Name three foods you can cook in a saucepan.
9. Describe how to cook your favorite dinner recipe.
10. (Cover the pictures.) Name six items used to cook or bake food in.

Expressive Activity
Read a recipe for French toast, stir-fry vegetables, a casserole, cookies, or muffins. Have the client talk about what cookware or bakeware items she would need to prepare the food.

Critical Thinking and Problem Solving
1. What could happen if you start cooking, but you don't have all your ingredients?
2. If soup boils over, what would you do?
3. If you smell something burning, what should you do?
4. If a pan catches on fire, what would you do?
5. How do you know what ingredients you will need to bake your favorite casserole?
6. How can you find out what ingredients you already have?
7. How do you know what to write on a shopping list?
8. How do you know when pancakes are ready to be flipped?
9. How can you tell if muffins are done baking?
10. How can you tell if cookies are done baking?

Vocabulary at Home: Kitchen – Cutting Utensils
Functional Vocabulary for Adolescents & Adults

Kitchen – Cutting Utensils

Receptive Vocabulary
Name each picture the client points to.

1. Point to the cutting board (vegetable peeler, grater, pizza cutter, knife, cheese cutter).
2. Show me which can cut pizza.
3. Which can cut cheese?
4. Which can grate carrots?
5. Which can cut celery?
6. Which can peel potatoes?
7. Which do you put your food on before cutting it?
8. Which are sharp?
9. Which do you have at school?
10. Which do you have at your home?

Receptive Activities
Before doing these activities, make two copies of the picture grid. Cut apart one grid to make picture cards.

1. Give the client the picture grid. Have him match the picture cards to the pictures on the grid. *Where is the _____?*
2. Place a real cutting board, knife, etc. on the table. Give a picture card to the client and have him put it by the matching item. *Find the _____.*
3. Prepare food, such as pizza, salad, or a quesadilla, using one or more of these cutting utensils. Have the client gather the items that you ask for.
4. Place the picture cards faceup on the table. Have the client follow your directions. *Touch the _____. Take the _____. Hand me the _____. Point to the _____. Turn over the _____.*
5. Cover three to six pictures on the picture grid. Show the client a picture card and have him tell you where it was on the picture grid. *Where was the _____?*
6. Use ads from a local store or a website that contains kitchen items. *Find a _____.*
7. Visit a kitchen or a store that sells kitchen items. Use the pictures as a shopping list. *Let's look for a _____.*

Word/Sentence Imitation and Sentence Completion
1. Ask the client to repeat each word after you say it. *Say _____.*
2. Use each word to complete the sentence *I cut with a _____.* Have the client repeat your sentences.
3. Print *I wash the _____* on a card. Have the client complete the sentence using the vocabulary words.

Expressive Vocabulary
1. Name each picture.
2. Which do you have at home?
3. What do you do with a _____?
4. How are a vegetable peeler and a cheese grater different?
5. Which of these utensils do you know how to use?
6. Name three food items you can cut with a knife.
7. Name three vegetables you can peel.
8. Name three foods that have grated cheese in or on them.
9. Describe how you would make a salad that has four different vegetables in it.
10. (Cover the pictures.) Name six cutting utensils.

Expressive Activity
Read a recipe for pizza, a quesadilla, a vegetable salad, or a fruit salad. Have the client talk about what utensils he would need to prepare the food.

Critical Thinking and Problem Solving
1. Why would you use a cutting board?
2. If a recipe asks for 1 cup of grated cheese, what do you do?
3. If a recipe asks for ½ cup chopped celery, what do you do?
4. If a recipe asks for 4 peeled potatoes, what do you do?
5. If a recipe asks for 6 slices of cheese, what do you do?
6. What is a safe way to hand a knife to another person?
7. What are some safety rules to remember when cutting food?
8. What would you do if you cut your finger?
9. Why is it important to follow kitchen safety rules?
10. How would you cut a pizza if four people want to share it?

Kitchen – Tableware

Receptive Vocabulary
Name each picture the client points to.

1. Point to the plate (spoon, bowl, fork, glass, knife).
2. Show me what holds a drink.
3. Which do you use for cutting?
4. Which do you use to eat cereal?
5. Which do you use to eat salad?
6. Which do you use to eat soup?
7. Which do you put food on?
8. Which are silverware?
9. Which do you have at your home?
10. Which would you see at a restaurant?

Receptive Activities
Before doing these activities, make two copies of the picture grid. Cut apart one grid to make picture cards.

1. Give the client the picture grid. Have her match the picture cards to the pictures on the grid. *Where is the _____?*
2. Place a real plate, bowl, glass, etc. on the table. Give a picture card to the client and have her put it by the matching item. *Find the _____.*
3. Place the picture cards faceup on the table. Have the client follow your directions. *Touch the _____. Take the _____. Hand me the _____. Point to the _____. Turn over the _____.*
4. Cover three to six pictures on the picture grid. Show the client a picture card and have her tell you where it was on the picture grid. *Where was the _____?*
5. Use ads from a local store or a website that contains kitchen items. *Find a _____.*
6. Visit a kitchen, a cafeteria, or a store that sells kitchen items. Use the pictures as a shopping list. *Let's look for a _____.*

Word/Sentence Imitation and Sentence Completion
1. Ask the client to repeat each word after you say it. *Say _____.*
2. Use each word to complete the sentence *I use a _____ when I eat.* Have the client repeat your sentences.
3. Print *I will wash the _____* on a card. Have the client complete the sentence using the vocabulary words.

Expressive Vocabulary
1. Name each picture.
2. What do all of these items have in common?
3. What do the dishes at your home look like?
4. Where do you keep these items?
5. Which have you used today?
6. Name three foods you eat with a spoon.
7. Name three drinks you could pour in a glass.
8. How are plates and paper plates the same? different?
9. Describe how you set the table.
10. (Cover the pictures.) Name six things used to set the table.

Expressive Activity
Have the client practice setting the table using these kitchen items. Ask her to talk about where she is placing each item.

Critical Thinking and Problem Solving
1. Which would you need to eat soup? salad? steak?
2. What do you do with your dishes when you're finished eating at home?
3. What do you do with your dishes when you're finished eating at a restaurant?
4. What would you do if you dropped your fork on the floor?
5. What would you do if the waiter at a restaurant forgot to give you silverware?
6. What would you do if you accidentally broke a glass?
7. If you worked as a busboy at a restaurant, what would your tasks be?
8. If you moved out on your own, what kitchen items would you need to buy?
9. How would you organize your kitchen drawers and cupboards?
10. How do you know if the dishes in a dishwasher are clean?

Vocabulary at Home: Kitchen – Utensils 1
Functional Vocabulary for Adolescents & Adults

Kitchen – Utensils 1

Receptive Vocabulary
Name each picture the client points to.

1. Point to the measuring spoons (mixer, mixing bowl, spatula, measuring cup, timer).
2. Show me which can measure salt.
3. Which can measure milk?
4. Which can mix ingredients together?
5. Which can flip pancakes?
6. Which can hold batter?
7. Which keeps track of a food's cooking time?
8. Which two measure ingredients?
9. Which do you have at home?
10. Which go in the kitchen?

Receptive Activities
Before doing these activities, make two copies of the picture grid. Cut apart one grid to make picture cards.

1. Give the client the picture grid. Have him match the picture cards to the pictures on the grid. *Where is/are the _____?*
2. Place a real measuring cup, timer, etc. on the table. Give a picture card to the client and have him put it by the matching item. *Find the _____.*
3. Prepare food, such as muffins, pancakes, or cookies, using one or more of these kitchen utensils. Have the client gather the items that you ask for.
4. Place the picture cards faceup on the table. Have the client follow your directions. *Touch the _____. Take the _____. Hand me the _____. Point to the _____. Turn over the _____.*
5. Cover three to six pictures on the picture grid. Show the client a picture card and have him tell you where it was on the picture grid. *Where was/were the _____?*
6. Use ads from a local store or a website that contains kitchen items. *Find (a) _____.*
7. Visit a kitchen or a store that sells kitchen items. Use the pictures as a shopping list. *Let's look for (a) _____.*

Word/Sentence Imitation and Sentence Completion
1. Ask the client to repeat each word after you say it. *Say _____.*
2. Use each word to complete the sentence *I use (a) _____.* Have the client repeat your sentences.
3. Print *Get the _____* on a card. Have the client complete the sentence using the vocabulary words.

Expressive Vocabulary
1. Name each picture.
2. What do all of these items have in common?
3. Which do you have at home?
4. Which have you used before?
5. What do you do with (a) _____?
6. How are measuring spoons and a measuring cup alike? different?
7. Name three food items that need to be stirred.
8. Name three foods you set a timer for while baking.
9. When would you use a mixer instead of a spoon?
10. (Cover the pictures.) Name six kitchen utensils.

Expressive Activity
Look at a recipe for muffins. Have the client talk about what items he would need to prepare the muffins.

Critical Thinking and Problem Solving
1. If a recipe says to bake for 12-15 minutes, how long should you set the timer for?
2. If a recipe says to bake for 20-25 minutes, what should you do?
3. If a recipe calls for 2 tablespoons of cinnamon, what do you do?
4. If a recipe calls for 1½ cups of flour, what do you do?
5. What should you do if the recipe makes two servings, but you need four servings?
6. What should you do if there's too much batter for the mixing bowl you're using?
7. Why should you preheat the oven before mixing the ingredients?
8. How could you learn to make a new food?
9. How do you know when cake batter has been mixed enough?
10. How do you know when muffins are done baking?

Kitchen – Utensils 2

Receptive Vocabulary
Name each picture the client points to.

1. Point to the colander (scraper, ladle, can opener, hot pad, oven mitt).
2. Show me which opens cans.
3. Which can scrape batter from a bowl?
4. Which is used to serve soup?
5. Which drains water from noodles?
6. Which protect your hands from hot pans?
7. Which have handles?
8. Which are stored in a drawer?
9. Which go in a kitchen?
10. Which do you have at home?

Receptive Activities
Before doing these activities, make two copies of the picture grid. Cut apart one grid to make picture cards.

1. Give the client the picture grid. Have her match the picture cards to the pictures on the grid. *Where is the _____?*
2. Place a real ladle, colander, etc. on the table. Give a picture card to the client and have her put it by the matching item. *Find the _____.*
3. Prepare food, such as spaghetti or other pasta, using one or more of these kitchen utensils. Have the client gather the items that you ask for.
4. Place the picture cards faceup on the table. Have the client follow your directions. *Touch the _____. Take the _____. Hand me the _____. Point to the _____. Turn over the _____.*
5. Cover three to six pictures on the picture grid. Show the client a picture card and have her tell you where it was on the picture grid. *Where was the _____?*
6. Use ads from a local store or a website that contains kitchen items. *Find a/an _____.*
7. Visit a kitchen or a store that sells kitchen items. Use the pictures as a shopping list. *Let's look for a/an _____.*

Word/Sentence Imitation and Sentence Completion
1. Ask the client to repeat each word after you say it. *Say _____.*
2. Use each word to complete the sentence *I use a/an _____.* Have the client repeat your sentences.
3. Print *I see a/an _____* on a card. Have the client complete the sentence using the vocabulary words.

Expressive Vocabulary
1. Name each picture.
2. What do all of these items have in common?
3. Which do you have at school?
4. Which do you have at home?
5. Which have you used before?
6. What do you do with a/an _____?
7. Why do people use hot pads and oven mitts?
8. Name three kinds of pasta that need to be strained.
9. How are an electric can opener and a manual can opener the same? different?
10. (Cover the pictures.) Name six kitchen utensils.

Expressive Activity
Read a recipe for spaghetti. Have the client talk about what utensils she would need to prepare and serve the pasta and the sauce.

Critical Thinking and Problem Solving
1. If a recipe says to bake for 8-10 minutes, what do you do?
2. What are some safety rules in the kitchen?
3. What do you do if your oven mitt or hot pad gets dirty?
4. If you moved into an apartment, what cooking supplies would you buy?
5. What foods would you like to learn how to cook?
6. Which do you prefer to use, a hot pad or an oven mitt?
7. After using a can opener to open a can, why should you be careful when removing the lid?
8. How would you organize these cooking utensils in your kitchen?
9. How can you tell if noodles are cooked?
10. How do you know if a pot of soup is hot?

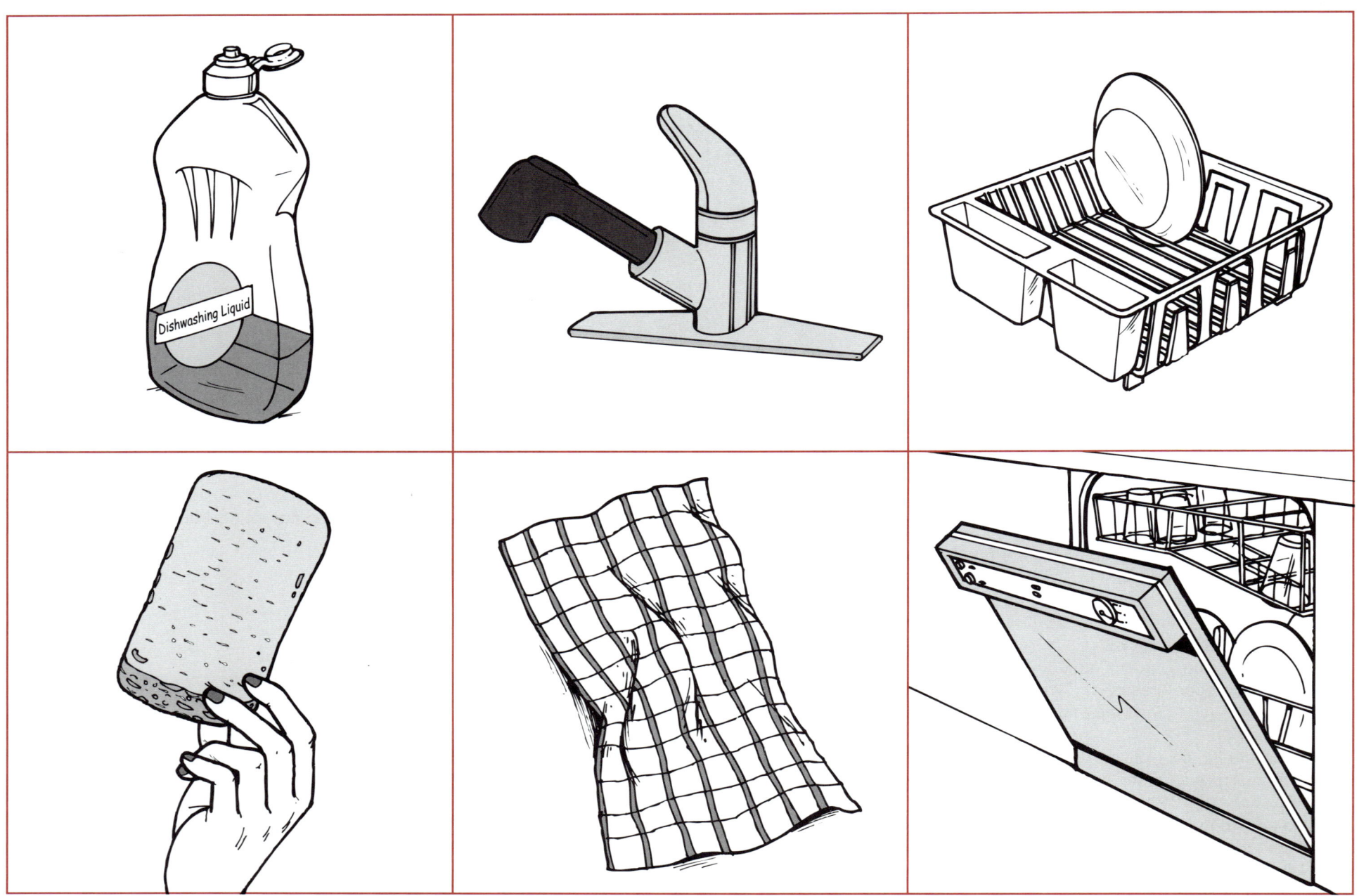

Vocabulary at Home: Kitchen – Washing Dishes
Functional Vocabulary for Adolescents & Adults

Kitchen – Washing Dishes

Receptive Vocabulary
Name each picture the client points to.

1. Point to the sponge (dishwasher, dish soap, faucet, dish towel, dish drainer).
2. Show me the machine that washes dishes.
3. Which do you use to turn on the water?
4. Which makes bubbles in the sink?
5. What do you use to scrub the dishes?
6. Where do you put wet dishes to dry?
7. Which do you use to dry the dishes?
8. Which do you have at school?
9. Which do you have at home?
10. Which would you see in a kitchen?

Receptive Activities
Before doing these activities, make two copies of the picture grid. Cut apart one grid to make picture cards.

1. Give the client the picture grid. Have him match the picture cards to the pictures on the grid. *Where is the _____?*
2. Visit a kitchen or a cafeteria. Put a piece of tape on a picture card and give it to the client. Have him place the card on the matching item as a label.
3. Wash dishes. Have the client follow directions that include the vocabulary words, such as *Turn on the faucet, Pour dish soap in the water, Get the sponge, Put the plate in the dish drainer,* and *Get the dish towel.*
4. Place the picture cards faceup on the table. Have the client follow your directions. *Touch the _____. Take the _____. Hand me the _____. Point to the _____. Turn over the _____.*
5. Cover three to six pictures on the picture grid. Show the client a picture card and have him tell you where it was on the picture grid. *Where was the _____?*
6. Use ads from a drug store or a grocery store. *Find (a) _____.*
7. Visit a drug store or a grocery store. Use the pictures as a shopping list. *Let's look for (a) _____.*

Word/Sentence Imitation and Sentence Completion
1. Ask the client to repeat each word after you say it. *Say _____.*
2. Use each word to complete the sentence *The _____ is in the kitchen.* Have the client repeat your sentences.
3. Print *I use (a) _____* on a card. Have the client complete the sentence using the vocabulary words.

Expressive Vocabulary
1. Name each picture.
2. What do all of these items have in common?
3. Which do you have at home?
4. What do you do with a sponge? towel? dish drainer?
5. What does a dishwasher do?
6. How often do you help with the dishes? What do you do?
7. Describe the steps to washing dishes in the sink.
8. Describe how to load and start a dishwasher.
9. Which do you prefer, washing dishes by hand or using a dishwasher? Why?
10. (Cover the pictures.) Name six items used to wash dishes.

Expressive Activity
Have the client teach someone how to wash and dry dishes. Ask the client to model and describe the actions before the other person takes a turn.

Critical Thinking and Problem Solving
1. What would you do if you ran out of dish soap?
2. What would you do if your dish towel smelled bad?
3. What would you do if you found a dirty plate in the cupboard?
4. What would you do if there were no more plates in the cupboard and it was time to eat?
5. What could you do if your sink got clogged?
6. Where would you look if you couldn't find the sponge?
7. When should you use the garbage disposal?
8. If you worked in a restaurant kitchen, what tasks might you do?
9. If you lived on your own, how would your dishes get cleaned?
10. Why is it a good idea to rinse the dishes before putting them in the dish drainer?

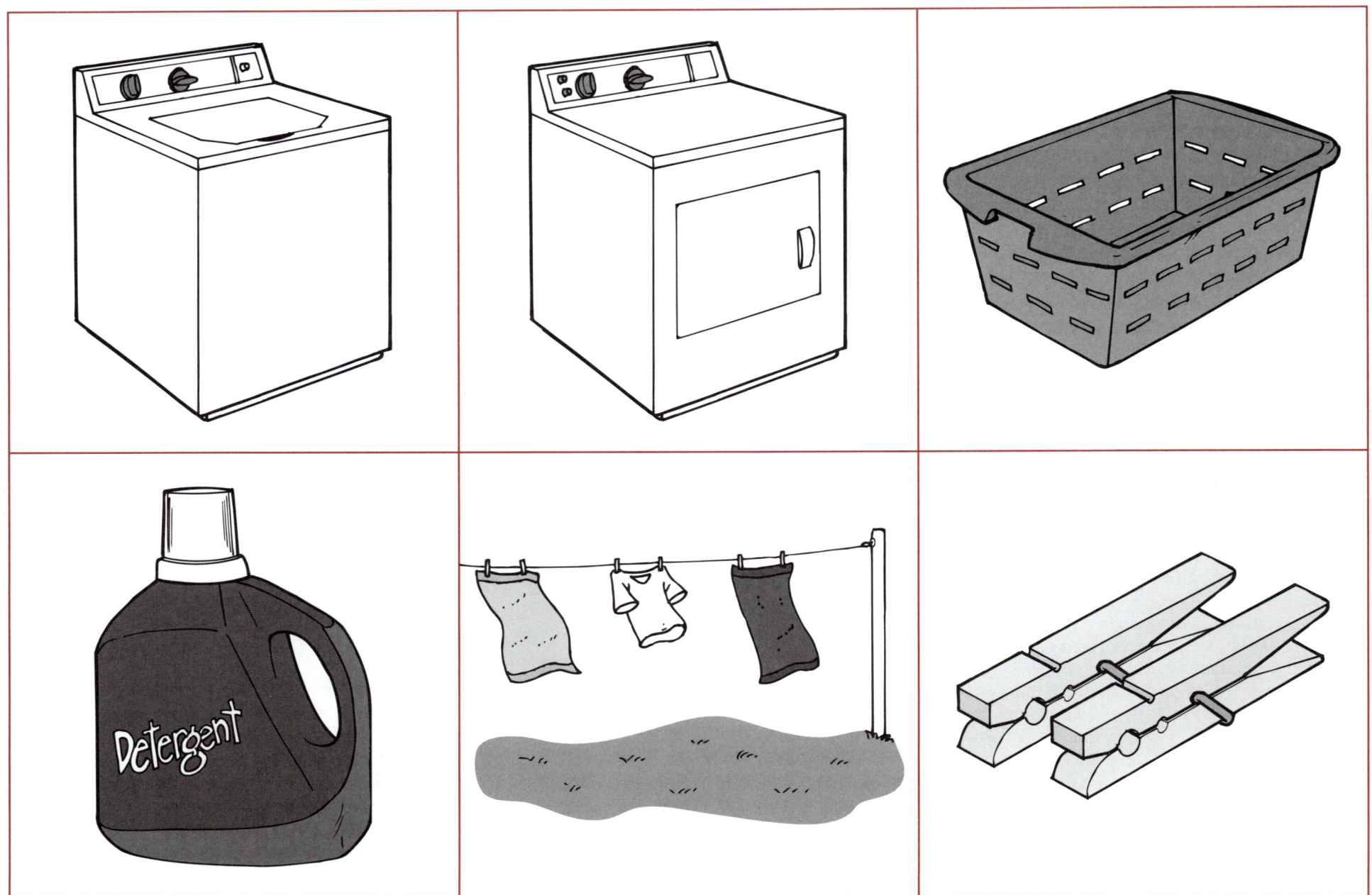

Vocabulary at Home: Laundry – Nouns

Laundry – Nouns

Receptive Vocabulary
Name each picture the client points to.

1. Point to the laundry basket (washer, clothespins, dryer, detergent, clothesline).
2. Show me which machine washes clothes.
3. Which machine dries clothes?
4. Which soap cleans clothes?
5. Where do people hang wet clothes?
6. Which do people use to fasten clothes to a clothesline?
7. Which do people use to carry clothes in?
8. Which do you have at your home?
9. Which do people take to the Laundromat?
10. Which are noisy?

Receptive Activities
Before doing these activities, make two copies of the picture grid. Cut apart one grid to make picture cards.

1. Give the client the picture grid. Have her match the picture cards to the pictures on the grid. *Where is the _____?*
2. Play a game of Bingo. Use pennies as markers.
3. Have the client practice doing laundry. Give directions using the vocabulary words. *Put this in the washing machine. Fill a cup with detergent. Put this in the dryer.*
4. Place the picture cards faceup on the table. Have the client follow your directions. *Touch the _____. Take the _____. Hand me the _____. Point to the _____. Turn over the _____.*
5. Cover three to six pictures on the picture grid. Show the client a picture card and have her tell you where it was on the picture grid. *Where was the _____?*
6. Use ads from a hardware store, appliance store, grocery store, or drug store. *Find (a) _____.*
7. Visit a Laundromat. Find items that match the pictures. *Let's look for (a) _____.*

Word/Sentence Imitation and Sentence Completion
1. Ask the client to repeat each word after you say it. *Say _____.*
2. Use each word to complete the sentence *I see (a) _____.* Have the client repeat your sentences.
3. Print *This is (a) _____* on a card. Have the client complete the sentence using the vocabulary words.

Expressive Vocabulary
1. Name each picture.
2. What do all of these items have in common?
3. What does a washing machine do?
4. What does a dryer do?
5. How are a dryer and a clothesline different?
6. How are a washing machine and a dryer different?
7. Which do you like better, a dryer or a clothesline? Why?
8. Who does the laundry at your home?
9. Describe how to do the laundry.
10. (Cover the pictures.) Name six things used to do laundry.

Expressive Activity
Have the client practice doing laundry. Ask her to use the vocabulary words to tell the steps involved in doing laundry.

Critical Thinking and Problem Solving
1. What kind of clothes should not go in the dryer?
2. After the dryer stops, what should you do if the clothes are still damp?
3. Which clothes need a "gentle" or "delicate" speed in the washer?
4. What would you like to get better at when doing laundry?
5. When should you use hot water in the washer? cold water?
6. When should you set the washer knob to "large load"? "small load"?
7. Why should you check clothing pockets before doing the laundry?
8. Why do people hang clothes on the clothesline?
9. How should you sort clothes before washing them?
10. How do you know when the washer is done?

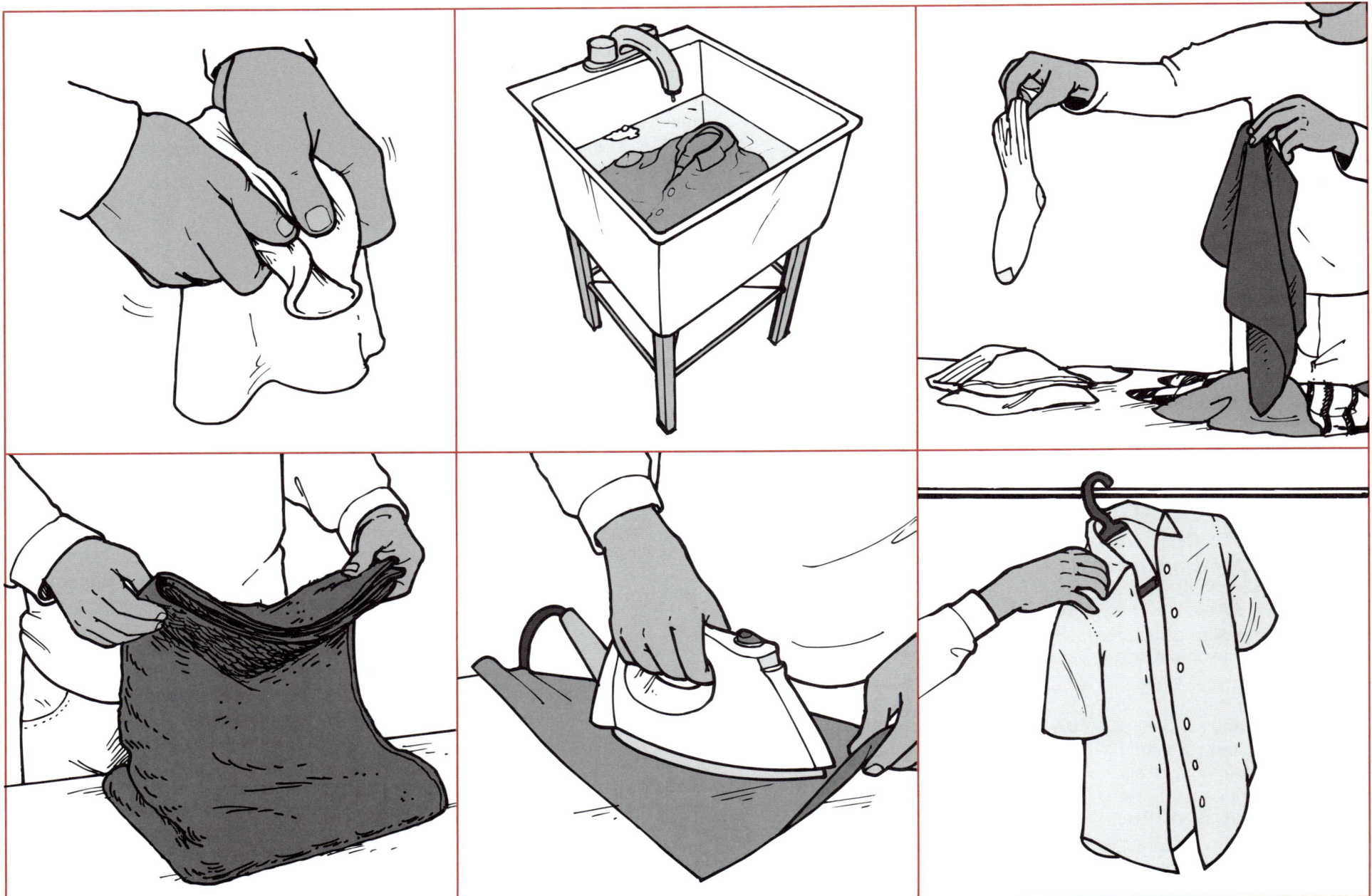

Vocabulary at Home: Laundry – Verbs

Laundry – Verbs

Receptive Vocabulary
Name each picture the client points to.

1. Point to hang (scrub, fold, soak, sort, iron).
2. Show me who is folding clothes.
3. Who is sorting laundry?
4. Who is scrubbing a stain?
5. Who is hanging clothes?
6. Who is ironing clothes?
7. Show me soaking clothes.
8. Which shows sorting clothes before washing them?
9. Which is used to get wrinkles out of clothing?
10. What do people do with a shirt before putting it in a closet? in a drawer?

Receptive Activities
Before doing these activities, make two copies of the picture grid. Cut apart one grid to make picture cards.

1. Give the client the picture grid. Have him match the picture cards to the pictures on the grid. *Who is _____?*
2. Play a game of Bingo. Use pennies as markers.
3. Have the client practice doing laundry. Give directions using the vocabulary words. *Scrub this stain. Sort these clothes. Fold these shorts. Hang these shirts.*
4. Play a pantomime game using the picture cards. Place six cards on the table and pantomime one of the actions. *What I am doing?*
5. Place the picture cards faceup on the table. Have the client follow your directions. *Touch _____. Take _____. Hand me _____. Point to _____. Turn over _____.*
6. Cover three to six pictures on the picture grid. Show the client a picture card and have him tell you where it was on the picture grid. *Where was _____?*

Word/Sentence Imitation and Sentence Completion
1. Ask the client to repeat each word after you say it. *Say _____.*
2. Use each word to complete the sentence *He is _____ clothes.* Have the client repeat your sentences.
3. Print *I like _____ clothes* on a card. Have the client complete the sentence using the vocabulary words.

Expressive Vocabulary
1. What is happening in each picture?
2. Describe what to do to a stain on clothing before washing the item.
3. Explain how to wash delicate clothes.
4. What clothes do you hang? fold?
5. Tell how to hang up a shirt. a pair of pants.
6. Explain how to fold a towel. a T-shirt.
7. Describe how to iron a shirt.
8. How do you decide which clothes to wash together?
9. Explain the steps in doing the laundry.
10. (Cover the pictures.) Name six things you can do with laundry.

Expressive Activity
Have the client practice doing laundry. Ask him to use the vocabulary words to tell the steps involved in doing laundry.

Critical Thinking and Problem Solving
1. What would happen if you mixed red and white clothes in the washing machine?
2. What clothes should not go in the washing machine?
3. What could happen to your clothes if the iron is set too hot?
4. What should you do if you burn your hand on the iron?
5. What could you do if your dress shirt keeps falling off the hanger?
6. If you worked at a clothing store, what tasks might you do?
7. If you worked in a hotel laundry room, what tasks might you do?
8. Why might you need to soak an item of clothing before washing it?
9. Why should you fold clothes after you wash and dry them?
10. Why do you need to be careful when handling an iron?

Vocabulary at Home: Nutrition – Breads & Grains

Nutrition – Breads & Grains

Receptive Vocabulary
Name each picture the client points to.

1. Point to the crackers (rice, pasta, tortillas, oatmeal, bread).
2. Show me which you would eat for breakfast.
3. Which would you eat for lunch?
4. Which would you eat for dinner?
5. Which is part of a sandwich?
6. Which is part of a burrito?
7. Which is another name for all types of noodles?
8. Which is salty?
9. Which are in the grain food group?
10. Which do you like to eat?

Receptive Activities
Before doing these activities, make two copies of the picture grid. Cut apart one grid to make picture cards.

1. Give the client a copy of the picture grid. Have him match the picture cards to the pictures on the grid. *Where is/are the _____?*
2. Prepare a meal that includes foods from the breads and grains food group, such as French toast or quesadillas. Have the client follow directions that include the vocabulary words.
3. Make a poster featuring various food items made from grains. Cut and paste pictures from grocery ads and magazines.
4. Cover three to six pictures on the picture grid. Show the client a picture card and have him tell you where it was on the picture grid. *Where was/were the _____?*
5. Look at a cookbook or a restaurant menu that has several pictures of foods that include ingredients from the breads and grains food group. *Find _____.*
6. Use ads from a grocery store. *Find _____.*
7. Visit a grocery store. Use the pictures as a shopping list. *Let's look for _____.*

Word/Sentence Imitation and Sentence Completion
1. Ask the client to repeat each word after you say it. *Say _____.*
2. Use each word to complete the sentence *Let's buy some _____.* Have the client repeat your sentences.
3. Print *I eat _____* on a card. Have the client complete the sentence using the vocabulary words.

Expressive Vocabulary
1. Name each picture.
2. What do all of these items have in common?
3. Name three sandwiches you could make with bread.
4. Name three foods you could make with tortillas.
5. Name three kinds of pasta.
6. Name three kinds of crackers.
7. Which of these could you eat for breakfast? lunch? dinner? snack?
8. What foods from the grain food group have you eaten today?
9. Describe how to cook rice.
10. (Cover the pictures.) Name six foods in the breads and grains food group.

Expressive Activity
Have the client brainstorm different kinds of breads, cereal, rice, and pasta that he likes to eat. Make a chart and list which could be eaten at breakfast, lunch, dinner, or snack time.

Critical Thinking and Problem Solving
1. Plan a breakfast that includes food from the breads and grains food group.
2. Plan a snack that includes food from the breads and grains food group.
3. Plan a lunch that includes food from the breads and grains food group.
4. Plan a dinner that includes food from the breads and grains food group.
5. What would you do if your box of crackers got crushed?
6. Why aren't donuts and cookies in the breads and grains food group?
7. How do you know if bread is fresh?
8. How do you know when pasta is done cooking?
9. How do you know when rice is done cooking?
10. How can you make sure you're eating enough healthy foods from the breads and grains food group each day?

Vocabulary at Home: Nutrition – Fruits
Functional Vocabulary for Adolescents & Adults

Nutrition – Fruits

Receptive Vocabulary
Name each picture the client points to.

1. Point to the banana (apple, applesauce, fruit cocktail, orange juice, orange).
2. Show me which you have for breakfast.
3. Which could you have for a snack?
4. Which could you have for lunch?
5. Which could you have for dinner?
6. Which need to be peeled?
7. Which can you eat with a spoon?
8. Which are fresh?
9. Which are in the fruit group?
10. Which do you like to eat?

Receptive Activities
Before doing these activities, make two copies of the picture grid. Cut apart one grid to make picture cards.

1. Give the client the picture grid. Have her match the picture cards to the pictures on the grid. *Where is the _____?*
2. Prepare a fruit salad. Have the client gather the ingredients and hand them to you as you need them.
3. Make a poster of different types of fruit. Cut and paste pictures from grocery ads and magazines.
4. Cover three to six pictures on the picture grid. Show the client a picture card and have her tell you where it was on the picture grid. *Where was the _____?*
5. Look at a restaurant menu that has several pictures in it. *See what fruits you can order.*
6. Use ads from a grocery store. *Find (a/an) _____.*
7. Visit a grocery store. Use the pictures as a shopping list. *Let's look for (a/an) _____.*

Word/Sentence Imitation and Sentence Completion
1. Ask the client to repeat each word after you say it. *Say _____.*
2. Use each word to complete the sentence *I will buy (a/an) _____.* Have the client repeat your sentences.
3. Print *I want (a/an) _____* on a card. Have the client complete the sentence using the vocabulary words.

Expressive Vocabulary
1. Name each picture.
2. Name three more fruits. Name three more kinds of juice.
3. What do all of these foods have in common?
4. What fruits would you put into a fruit salad?
5. Which of these are fresh fruits? canned?
6. Which could you have for breakfast? lunch? dinner? snack?
7. Where do you keep each item?
8. Describe each item.
9. How are an apple and a banana the same? different?
10. (Cover the pictures.) Name six foods in the fruit food group.

Expressive Activity
Have the client sample different fruits and then talk about which ones she likes and dislikes.

Critical Thinking and Problem Solving
1. Plan a breakfast that includes fruit.
2. Plan a snack that includes fruit.
3. Plan a lunch that includes fruit.
4. Plan a dinner that includes fruit.
5. What would you do if you spilled your orange juice?
6. What size container would you put fruit cocktail in to bring in your lunch bag?
7. What size container would you put applesauce in to serve your family?
8. How do you choose bananas at the store?
9. How do you choose apples at the store?
10. How can you make sure you're eating enough healthy foods from the fruit food group each day?

Nutrition – Meat & Protein

Receptive Vocabulary
Name each picture the client points to.

1. Point to the hamburgers (eggs, chicken, peanut butter, hot dogs, refried beans).
2. Show me which you could eat for breakfast.
3. Which could you eat for lunch?
4. Which could you eat for dinner?
5. Which could be in a sandwich?
6. Which can be in a burrito?
7. Which go in buns?
8. Which are in the meat and protein food group?
9. Which are served hot? cold?
10. Which do you like to eat?

Receptive Activities
Before doing these activities, make two copies of the picture grid. Cut apart one grid to make picture cards.

1. Give the client the picture grid. Have him match the picture cards to the pictures on the grid. *Where is/are the _____?*
2. Prepare a meal that includes foods from the meat and protein food group, such as hot dogs, eggs, or a bean burrito. Have the client follow directions that include the vocabulary words.
3. Make a poster featuring meat, beans, and protein. Cut and paste pictures from grocery ads and magazines.
4. Cover three to six pictures on the picture grid. Show the client a picture card and have him tell you where it was on the picture grid. *Where was/were the _____?*
5. Look at a cookbook or a restaurant menu that has several pictures of foods from the meat and protein food group. *Find _____.*
6. Use ads from a grocery store. *Find _____.*
7. Visit a grocery store. Use the pictures as a shopping list. *Let's look for _____.*

Word/Sentence Imitation and Sentence Completion
1. Ask the client to repeat each word after you say it. *Say _____.*
2. Use each word to complete the sentence *Let's buy some _____.* Have the client repeat your sentences.
3. Print *I eat _____* on a card. Have the client complete the sentence using the vocabulary words.

Expressive Vocabulary
1. Name each picture.
2. Name three meals with chicken.
3. Name three ways to cook eggs.
4. What do all of these foods have in common?
5. Which come from animals? plants?
6. Where do you keep each food?
7. Which could you eat for breakfast? lunch? dinner? snack?
8. Describe each food item.
9. Describe how to make a peanut butter and jelly sandwich.
10. (Cover the pictures.) Name six foods in the meat and protein food group.

Expressive Activity
Have the client sample different kinds of sliced meat and then talk about which ones he likes and dislikes.

Critical Thinking and Problem Solving
1. Plan a breakfast that includes a meat or protein.
2. Plan a snack that includes a meat or protein.
3. Plan a lunch that includes a meat or protein.
4. Plan a dinner that includes a meat or protein.
5. What would you do if you were out of peanut butter and wanted to make a sandwich?
6. When grocery shopping, why should you open the egg carton and check the eggs before buying them?
7. Why is it a good idea to keep meat, chicken, and eggs in the refrigerator?
8. How do you know if meat is fresh?
9. How do you know when a hamburger is done cooking?
10. How can you make sure you're eating enough healthy foods from the meat and protein food group each day?

Vocabulary at Home: Nutrition – Milk, Yogurt, & Cheese
Functional Vocabulary for Adolescents & Adults

Nutrition – Milk, Yogurt, & Cheese

Receptive Vocabulary
Name each picture the client points to.

1. Point to the cheese (cottage cheese, ice cream, milk, pudding, yogurt).
2. Show me which you would eat at breakfast.
3. Which could you have for a snack?
4. Which could you have for lunch?
5. Which could you have for dinner?
6. Which could you eat for dessert?
7. Which is made with milk?
8. Which do you drink? eat?
9. Which must be kept cold?
10. Which do you like to eat?

Receptive Activities
Before doing these activities, make two copies of the picture grid. Cut apart one grid to make picture cards.

1. Give the client a copy of the picture grid. Have her match the picture cards to the pictures on the grid. *Where is the _____?*
2. Prepare a meal that includes foods from the milk, yogurt, and cheese food group, such as hot chocolate, quesadillas, or a grilled cheese sandwich. Have the client follow directions that include the vocabulary words.
3. Make a poster featuring dairy products. Cut and paste pictures from grocery ads and magazines.
4. Cover three to six pictures on the picture grid. Show the client a picture card and have her tell you where it was on the picture grid. *Where was the _____?*
5. Look at a cookbook or a restaurant menu that has several pictures of foods that include ingredients from the milk, yogurt, and cheese food group. *Find _____.*
6. Use ads from a grocery store. *Find _____.*
7. Visit a grocery store. Use the pictures as a shopping list. *Let's look for _____.*

Word/Sentence Imitation and Sentence Completion
1. Ask the client to repeat each word after you say it. *Say _____.*
2. Use each word to complete the sentence *Let's buy some _____.* Have the client repeat your sentences.
3. Print *I eat _____* on a card. Have the client complete the sentence using the vocabulary words.

Expressive Vocabulary
1. Name each picture.
2. Name three foods that have cheese in them.
3. Name three yogurt flavors. Name three ice-cream flavors.
4. What do all of these foods have in common?
5. Which do you keep in the refrigerator? freezer?
6. Which could you eat for breakfast? lunch? dinner? snack?
7. What foods from the milk, yogurt, and cheese group have you eaten today?
8. Where could you buy each item?
9. Describe each dairy product.
10. (Cover the pictures.) Name six foods in the milk, yogurt, and cheese food group.

Expressive Activity
Have the client brainstorm different foods from the milk, yogurt, and cheese food group that she likes to eat. Make a chart that lists which could be eaten at breakfast, lunch, dinner, or snack time.

Critical Thinking and Problem Solving
1. Plan a breakfast that includes food from the milk, yogurt, and cheese food group.
2. Plan a snack that includes food from the milk, yogurt, and cheese food group.
3. Plan a lunch that includes food from the milk, yogurt, and cheese food group.
4. Plan a dinner that includes food from the milk, yogurt, and cheese food group.
5. What would you do if your milk smelled sour?
6. What would you do if your cheese had mold on it?
7. What would you do if your ice cream melted?
8. Why is it a good idea to keep milk, yogurt, and cheese in the refrigerator?
9. Why is it a good idea to look at the dates stamped on your milk and yogurt?
10. How can you make sure you're eating enough healthy foods from the milk, yogurt, and cheese food group each day?

Nutrition – Vegetables

Receptive Vocabulary
Name each picture the client points to.

1. Point to the lettuce (carrots, broccoli, peas, vegetable soup, corn on the cob).
2. Show me what you could eat for lunch.
3. Which could you eat for dinner?
4. Which are fresh?
5. Which is frozen?
6. Which is canned?
7. Which are green?
8. Which are served hot?
9. Which are in the vegetable food group?
10. Which do you like to eat?

Receptive Activities
Before doing these activities, make two copies of the picture grid. Cut apart one grid to make picture cards.

1. Give the client the picture grid. Have him match the picture cards to the pictures on the grid. *Where is/are the _____?*
2. Prepare a vegetable salad or vegetable soup. Have the client gather the ingredients that you ask for.
3. Make a poster featuring vegetables. Cut and paste pictures from grocery ads and magazines.
4. Cover three to six pictures on the picture grid. Show the client a picture card and have him tell you where it was on the picture grid. *Where was/were the _____?*
5. Look at a restaurant menu that has several pictures in it. *See what vegetables you can order.*
6. Use ads from a grocery store. *Find _____.*
7. Visit a grocery store. Use the pictures as a shopping list. *Let's look for _____.*

Word/Sentence Imitation and Sentence Completion
1. Ask the client to repeat each word after you say it. *Say _____.*
2. Use each word to complete the sentence *I want some _____.* Have the client repeat your sentences.
3. Print *I eat _____* on a card. Have the client complete the sentence using the vocabulary words.

Expressive Vocabulary
1. Name each picture.
2. What do all of these foods have in common?
3. What is the difference between frozen and fresh vegetables?
4. What is the difference between canned and fresh vegetables?
5. Which vegetables could you eat for lunch? dinner? snack?
6. Where do you keep each item?
7. Where in a grocery store would you find each item?
8. Describe each item.
9. Describe how to make a salad.
10. (Cover the pictures.) Name six foods in the vegetable food group.

Expressive Activity
Have the client sample different vegetables, perhaps raw with dip, and then talk about which ones he likes and dislikes. You could also cook frozen peas and canned peas, and have the client discuss which ones he likes better.

Critical Thinking and Problem Solving
1. Plan a snack that includes a vegetable.
2. Plan a lunch that includes a vegetable.
3. Plan a dinner that includes a vegetable.
4. What would you do if you ran out of salad dressing and wanted to eat a salad?
5. What would you do if you couldn't find the canned vegetables at the store?
6. What would you do if the server at a restaurant forgot to bring your salad?
7. Why is it a good idea to keep fresh vegetables in the refrigerator?
8. How do you know if your vegetable soup is hot?
9. How do you know if your lettuce is fresh?
10. How can you make sure you're eating enough healthy foods from the vegetable food group each day?

Vocabulary at Home: What's for Breakfast?
Functional Vocabulary for Adolescents & Adults

What's for Breakfast?

Receptive Vocabulary
Name each picture the client points to.

1. Point to the pancakes (cereal, sausage, bacon, waffle, eggs).
2. Show me which go with syrup.
3. What goes with milk?
4. Which are meats?
5. Which do you eat with a fork?
6. Which do you eat with a spoon?
7. Which do you eat for breakfast?
8. Which could you order at a restaurant?
9. Which are sweet?
10. Which do you like to eat?

Receptive Activities
Before doing these activities, make two copies of the picture grid. Cut apart one grid to make picture cards.

1. Give the client the picture grid. Have her match the picture cards to the pictures on the grid. *Where is/are the _____?*
2. Prepare one or more of these breakfast foods. Ask the client to gather the items that you ask for.
3. Place the picture cards faceup on the table. Have the client follow your directions. *Touch the _____. Take the _____. Hand me the _____. Point to the _____. Turn over the _____.*
4. Cover three to six pictures on the picture grid. Show the client a picture card and have her tell you where it was on the picture grid. *Where was/were the _____?*
5. Look at a cookbook that has several pictures of breakfast foods in it. *Find (a) _____.*
6. Look at a restaurant menu that has several pictures of breakfast foods in it. *Find (a) _____.*
7. Visit a grocery store. Use the pictures as a shopping list. *Let's look for (a) _____.*

Word/Sentence Imitation and Sentence Completion
1. Ask the client to repeat each word after you say it. *Say _____.*
2. Use each word to complete the sentence *I like (a) _____ for breakfast.* Have the client repeat your sentences.
3. Print *I eat (a) _____* on a card. Have the client complete the sentence using the vocabulary words.

Expressive Vocabulary
1. Name each picture.
2. What do all of these items have in common?
3. Which are served hot? cold?
4. Which are in the meat group?
5. Which are in the bread group?
6. What restaurants serve breakfast?
7. Name three kinds of cereal. Which kind do you like best?
8. Name three ways eggs are cooked. Which way do you like best?
9. Describe each breakfast food.
10. (Cover the pictures.) Name six breakfast foods.

Expressive Activity
Have the client role-play ordering breakfast at a restaurant using a menu. (Restaurants will often donate menus when asked.)

Critical Thinking and Problem Solving
1. What would you do if you ordered pancakes at a restaurant, but the server brought you waffles?
2. What would you do if the server forgot to bring you syrup?
3. When putting away groceries, where would you put eggs, bacon, and sausage?
4. When putting away groceries, where would you put frozen waffles?
5. When putting away groceries, where would you put pancake mix and cereal?
6. Why should some foods go in the refrigerator?
7. How do you know when pancakes are done cooking?
8. How do you know when sausage is done cooking?
9. How do you know if your breakfast is healthy?
10. Create a healthy breakfast menu that contains four food groups.

Vocabulary at Home: What's for Dinner?

What's for Dinner?

Receptive Vocabulary
Name each picture the client points to.

1. Point to the spaghetti (fish, egg rolls, macaroni and cheese, chicken, enchiladas).
2. Show me which are made with noodles.
3. Which are meat or are made with meat?
4. Which would you eat with a fork?
5. Which could you pick up to eat?
6. Which could be spicy?
7. Which do you eat at home?
8. Which could you eat at school?
9. Which could you eat at a restaurant?
10. Which do you like to eat?

Receptive Activities
Before doing these activities, make two copies of the picture grid. Cut apart one grid to make picture cards.

1. Give the client the picture grid. Have her match the picture cards to the pictures on the grid. *Where is/are the _____?*
2. Prepare one of these dinners. Ask the client to gather the items that you ask for.
3. Place the picture cards faceup on the table. Have the client follow your directions. *Touch the _____. Take the _____. Hand me the _____. Point to the _____. Turn over the _____.*
4. Cover three to six pictures on the picture grid. Show the client a picture card and have her tell you where it was on the picture grid. *Where was/were the _____?*
5. Look at a cookbook or a restaurant menu that has several pictures of dinner foods in it. *Find (an) _____.*
6. Use ads from a grocery store. *Find the ingredients to make (an) _____.*
7. Visit a grocery store. Use the pictures as a shopping list. *Let's look for (an) _____.*

Word/Sentence Imitation and Sentence Completion
1. Ask the client to repeat each word after you say it. *Say _____.*
2. Use each word to complete the sentence *I like (an) _____.* Have the client repeat your sentences.
3. Print *I eat (an) _____* on a card. Have the client complete the sentence using the vocabulary words.

Expressive Vocabulary
1. Name each picture.
2. What do all of these items have in common?
3. What restaurants have you eaten dinner at?
4. Which can you order at a restaurant?
5. Which do you like to eat?
6. Which do you know how to make?
7. How do you make macaroni and cheese?
8. How are spaghetti and macaroni and cheese different?
9. Describe each dinner food.
10. (Cover the pictures.) Name six dinner foods.

Expressive Activity
Have the client role-play ordering dinner at a restaurant using a menu. (Restaurants will often donate menus when asked.)

Critical Thinking and Problem Solving
1. What if you ordered spaghetti but the server brought you macaroni and cheese?
2. What would you do if the chicken you ordered at a restaurant was cold?
3. When putting away groceries, where would you put macaroni noodles and a jar of spaghetti sauce?
4. When putting away groceries, where you put chicken breasts and fresh fish?
5. When putting away groceries, where would you put vegetables and tortillas?
6. If you were having people over for dinner, which foods would you serve? Why?
7. How do you know when macaroni noodles are done cooking?
8. How do you know when chicken is done cooking?
9. What healthy side dishes could go with these dinner entrees?
10. Create a healthy dinner menu that contains four food groups.

What's for Lunch?

Receptive Vocabulary
Name each picture the client points to.

1. Point to the grilled cheese sandwich (hamburger, pizza, ham sandwich, chicken strips, taco).
2. Show me which are sandwiches.
3. Which are hot?
4. Which are cold?
5. Which have cheese?
6. Which have lettuce?
7. Which do you eat at home?
8. Which could you eat at school?
9. Which could you order at a restaurant?
10. Which do you like to eat?

Receptive Activities
Before doing these activities, make two copies of the picture grid. Cut apart one grid to make picture cards.

1. Give the client the picture grid. Have him match the picture cards to the pictures on the grid. *Where is/are the _____?*
2. Prepare one of these lunch items. Ask the client to gather the items you ask for.
3. Place the picture cards faceup on the table. Have the client follow your directions. *Touch the _____. Take the _____. Hand me the _____. Point to the _____. Turn over the _____.*
4. Cover three to six pictures on the picture grid. Show the client a picture card and have him tell you where it was on the picture grid. *Where was/were the _____?*
5. Look at a cookbook that has several pictures of lunch foods in it. *Find (a) _____.*
6. Look at a restaurant menu that has several pictures of lunch foods in it. *Find (a) _____.*
7. Visit a grocery store. Use the pictures as a shopping list. *Let's look for (a) _____.*

Word/Sentence Imitation and Sentence Completion
1. Ask the client to repeat each word after you say it. *Say _____.*
2. Use each word to complete the sentence *I'd like (a) _____.* Have the client repeat your sentences.
3. Print *I eat (a) _____* on a card. Have the client complete the sentence using the vocabulary words.

Expressive Vocabulary
1. Name each picture.
2. What do all of these items have in common?
3. Describe each lunch food.
4. Which can you buy in the cafeteria?
5. Which can you buy at a fast-food restaurant?
6. Which could you bring in a sack lunch?
7. What will/did you have for lunch today?
8. Which do you know how to make?
9. How do you make a grilled cheese sandwich?
10. (Cover the pictures.) Name six lunch foods.

Expressive Activity
Have the client role-play ordering lunch at a restaurant using a menu. (Restaurants will often donate menus when asked.)

Critical Thinking and Problem Solving
1. What would you do if you ordered a pepperoni pizza but you got cheese?
2. What would you do if the cashier forgot to give you the sauce for your chicken strips?
3. When putting away groceries, where would you put cheese, lettuce, and ground beef?
4. When putting away groceries, where would you put a loaf of bread and taco shells?
5. How could you find out what ingredients you need to make tacos?
6. How could you figure out what you need to buy to make pizza?
7. How would you order a hamburger if you don't like onions?
8. How would you order a taco if you don't want the cheese?
9. How do you plan a healthy lunch?
10. Create a healthy lunch menu that includes four food groups.

Vocabulary in the Community: Apartment
Functional Vocabulary for Adolescents & Adults

Apartment

Receptive Vocabulary
Name each picture the client points to.

1. Point to the tenant (balcony, rent, apartment, landlord, roommate).
2. Which is a place to live?
3. Who lives in an apartment?
4. Who lives with a tenant?
5. Who does a tenant pay?
6. Which does a tenant pay?
7. Which is outside the apartment and has a rail around it?
8. Where would you find a couch?
9. Where could you find potted plants?
10. Who are the people?

Receptive Activities
Before doing these activities, make two copies of the picture grid. Cut apart one grid to make picture cards.

1. Give the client the picture grid. Have her match the picture cards to the pictures on the grid. *Where is the _____?*
2. Play a game of Bingo. Use pennies as markers.
3. Place the picture cards faceup on the table. Have the client follow your directions. *Touch the _____. Take the _____. Hand me the _____. Point to the _____. Turn over the _____.*
4. Cover three to six pictures on the picture grid. Show the client a picture card and have her tell you where it was on the picture grid. *Where was the _____?*
5. Use the classified section of your local newspaper or look on websites to find pictures of apartments for rent. *Find apartments. Find balconies. How much is the rent?*
6. Visit a local apartment complex. *Let's look for (a/an) _____.*

Word/Sentence Imitation and Sentence Completion
1. Ask the client to repeat each word after you say it. *Say _____.*
2. Use each word to complete the sentence *Here is (a/an) _____.* Have the client repeat your sentences.
3. Print *I see (a/an) _____* on a card. Have the client complete the sentence using the vocabulary words.

Expressive Vocabulary
1. Name each picture.
2. What do all of these items have in common?
3. How is an apartment like a house?
4. Describe a balcony.
5. What does a tenant do?
6. What does a landlord do?
7. What is rent?
8. What is a roommate?
9. Describe your home.
10. Describe where you would like to live as an adult.

Expressive Activity
Use the classified section of your local newspaper to look for apartments for rent. Discuss features like the location and number of bedrooms, and how much the rent is, who could be a roommate, what transportation is available, and what furniture the client would use.

Critical Thinking and Problem Solving
1. What features would you want your apartment to have?
2. What features would you want your apartment complex to have?
3. What are the advantages of having a roommate?
4. What are the disadvantages of having a roommate?
5. If you lived in an apartment, what would you do about cooking meals? cleaning? laundry?
6. What do you need to learn to do better in order to live in an apartment?
7. Where would you look to find an apartment that you liked and that you could afford?
8. Who would you call if your apartment had a leaky faucet?
9. How would you get from your apartment to work?
10. How would you earn enough money to pay rent?

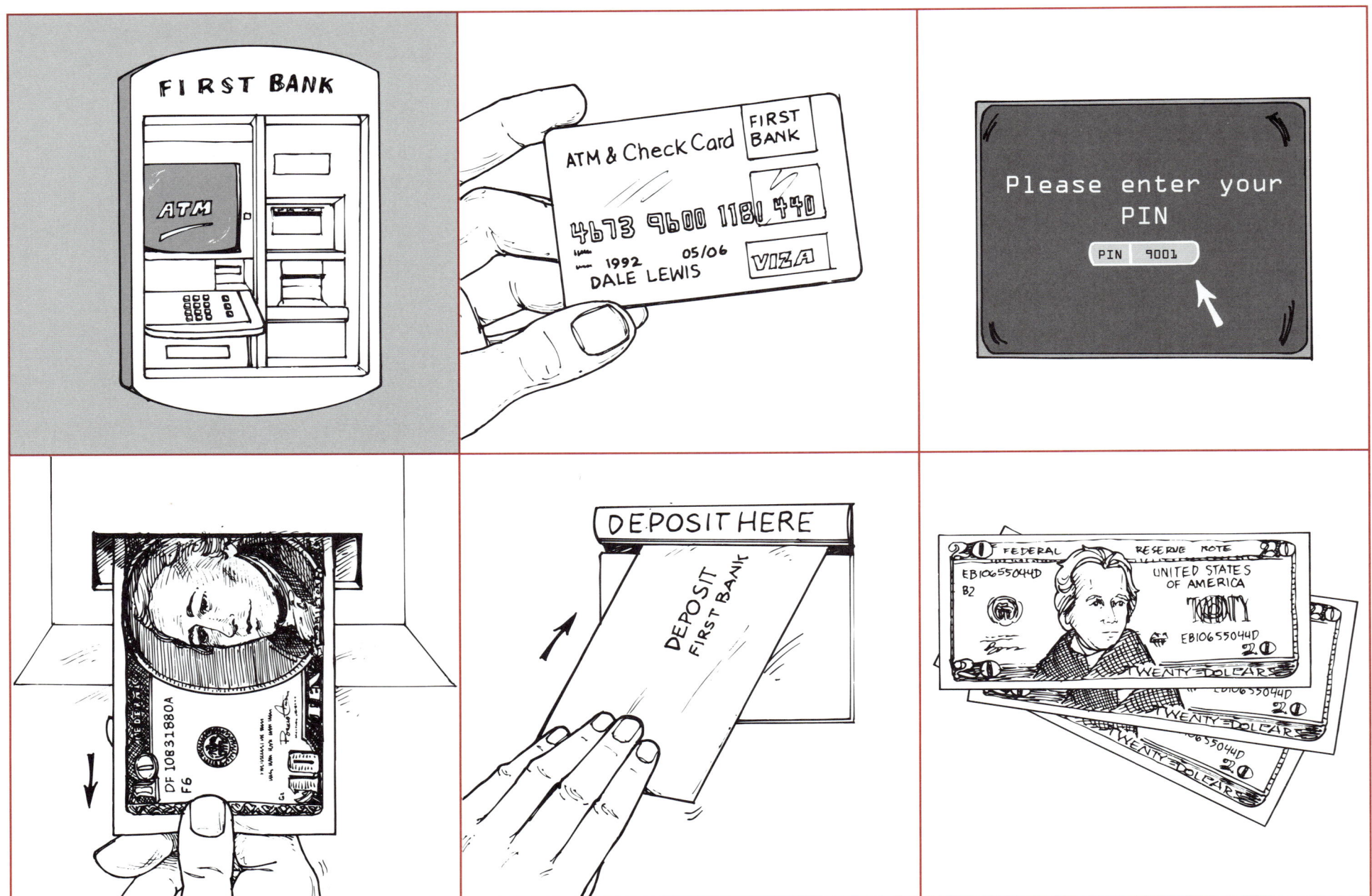

Vocabulary in the Community: ATM (Automated Teller Machine)
Functional Vocabulary for Adolescents & Adults

ATM (Automated Teller Machine)

Receptive Vocabulary
Name each picture the client points to.

1. Point to the Personal Identification Number/PIN (cash, Automated Teller Machine/ATM, withdrawal, ATM card, deposit).
2. Which is an ATM (Automated Teller Machine)?
3. Which is money that you put in the ATM?
4. Which is money that you take out of the ATM?
5. Which is an ATM card?
6. Which is cash?
7. Which is a PIN (Personal Identification Number)?
8. Which do you keep in your wallet?
9. Which should you record in your checkbook?
10. Which do you need to get cash from the ATM?

Receptive Activities
Before doing these activities, make two copies of the picture grid. Cut apart one grid to make picture cards.

1. Give the client the picture grid. Have him match the picture cards to the pictures on the grid. *Where is the _____?*
2. Play a game of Bingo. Use pennies as markers.
3. Place the picture cards faceup on the table. Have the client follow your directions. *Touch the _____. Take the _____. Hand me the _____. Point to the _____. Turn over the _____.*
4. Cover three to six pictures on the picture grid. Show the client a picture card and have him tell you where it was on the picture grid. *Where was the _____?*
5. Role-play how to use an ATM card to deposit and withdraw money. Using the vocabulary words, give the clients directions to follow throughout the activity. *Get out your ATM card. Put it in the ATM. Punch in your PIN number.*
6. Visit a local ATM to make a deposit or a withdrawal. Using the vocabulary words, give the client directions to follow.

Word/Sentence Imitation and Sentence Completion
1. Ask the client to repeat each word after you say it. *Say _____.*
2. Use each word to complete the sentence *This is (a/an) _____.* Have the client repeat your sentences.
3. Print *I see (a/an) _____* on a card. Have the client complete the sentence using the vocabulary words.

Expressive Vocabulary
1. Name each picture.
2. What do these pictures have in common?
3. Where can you find an ATM?
4. What do you do with an ATM card?
5. What do you do when the ATM asks for your PIN?
6. Describe how to deposit a check using an ATM.
7. Tell how to withdraw cash using an ATM.
8. What is the difference between a deposit and a withdrawal?
9. What should you write in your checkbook register?
10. (Cover the pictures.) Name six words related to banking with an ATM.

Expressive Activity
Role-play getting a bank account and an ATM card. Have the client fill out an application for practice, and role-play meeting with a bank teller.

Critical Thinking and Problem Solving
1. What might happen if you don't record your ATM transactions in your checkbook register?
2. While waiting to use an ATM, why shouldn't you stand right behind a person using the ATM?
3. What would you do with your monthly bank statement?
4. What should you do if you lose your ATM card?
5. Where is a good place to keep your ATM card?
6. Where is a good place to keep your PIN?
7. Why is it a good idea to keep your PIN a secret?
8. How can you check to see if your check register is correct?
9. How can you find out how much money is in your bank account?
10. When making a withdrawal, why is it a good idea to count the money you get from the ATM?

Bank

Receptive Vocabulary
Name each picture the client points to.

1. Point to the wallet (teller, checkbook register, withdrawal, checkbook, deposit).
2. Where can you store your money?
3. Where can you store your checks and your checkbook register?
4. Who works at a bank?
5. Which is money that you put in a bank?
6. Which is money that you take out of a bank?
7. Which shows how much money you have in your checkbook?
8. Who can tell you about your bank account?
9. Which shows what you can do with your paycheck at a bank?
10. Where do you write deposits and withdrawals you've made to your checking account?

Receptive Activities
Before doing these activities, make two copies of the picture grid. Cut apart one grid to make picture cards.

1. Give the client the picture grid. Have her match the picture cards to the pictures on the grid. *Where is the _____?*
2. Place the picture cards faceup on the table. Have the client follow your directions. *Touch the _____. Take the _____. Hand me the _____. Point to the _____. Turn over the _____.*
3. Cover three to six pictures on the picture grid. Show the client a picture card and have her tell you where it was on the picture grid. *Where was the _____?*
4. Role-play going to a bank to make a deposit or withdrawal. Have one client be the teller and the other clients be the customers. Use pretend cash and checks, and record the transactions on a checkbook register. Using the vocabulary words, give the clients directions to follow throughout the activity. *Get out your checkbook. Take the money you want to deposit out of your wallet. Hand it to the teller.*
5. Visit a local bank to make a deposit or a withdrawal. Using the vocabulary words, give the client directions to follow.

Word/Sentence Imitation and Sentence Completion
1. Ask the client to repeat each word after you say it. *Say _____.*
2. Use each word to complete the sentence *Here is a _____.* Have the client repeat your sentences.
3. Print *That is a _____* on a card. Have the client complete the sentence using the vocabulary words.

Expressive Vocabulary
1. Name each picture.
2. What does this person and all of these items have in common?
3. Name a bank.
4. What does a bank teller do?
5. Describe how to withdraw money from a bank.
6. Tell how to deposit money at a bank.
7. Explain how to write a check.
8. Describe what to write in a checkbook register.
9. Tell how to balance a checkbook.
10. (Cover the pictures.) Name six items or people you would see at a bank.

Expressive Activity
Have the clients role-play going to a bank teller to withdraw money from their checking accounts. Ask the client who plays the bank teller to describe her job and what she would say when helping a customer. Have the customers describe what they need to do to withdraw money and what they should say to the teller. The customers should show a bank number and ID, put the money in a wallet, and record the transaction in a checkbook register.

Critical Thinking and Problem Solving
1. What could happen if you forget to record a check you write in your checkbook register?
2. What should you do with your monthly bank statement?
3. What can you do to avoid bouncing a check?
4. What could you do if you run out of checks?
5. What should you do if you lose your checkbook? wallet?
6. Where is a good place to keep your checkbook? wallet?
7. How could you find out if you have enough money in your account to write a check?
8. How can you prevent bouncing a check?
9. Why do store clerks ask for the person's ID when they accept checks?
10. Why do people keep money in banks?

City Bus

Receptive Vocabulary
Name each picture the client points to.

1. Point to the bus schedule (ID card, route number, bus stop, bus fare, bus driver).
2. Where do you wait for a city bus?
3. Which do you show the bus driver?
4. Which do you pay to ride a city bus?
5. Who drives a city bus?
6. Which number shows which bus it is?
7. Which lists the times the bus will come?
8. Which do you bring on the bus?
9. Who wears a uniform?
10. Which have you seen before?

Receptive Activities
Before doing these activities, make two copies of the picture grid. Cut apart one grid to make picture cards.

1. Give the client the picture grid. Have him match the picture cards to the pictures on the grid. *Where is the _____?*
2. Play a game of Bingo. Use pennies as markers.
3. Place the picture cards faceup on the table. Have the client follow your directions. *Touch the _____. Take the _____. Hand me the _____. Point to the _____. Turn over the _____.*
4. Cover three to six pictures on the picture grid. Show the client a picture card and have him tell you where it was on the picture grid. *Where was the _____?*
5. Role-play boarding a city bus. Make a bus stop sign and post it by some chairs for a bus stop. Line up other chairs as if they were seats on a bus. Ask one client to be the bus driver and the other clients to be the riders. Using the vocabulary words, give the clients directions to follow throughout the activity. *Wait at the bus stop. Get out your bus fare. Get out your ID card.*
6. Take a city bus to a desirable location. Using the vocabulary words, give the client directions to follow.

Word/Sentence Imitation and Sentence Completion
1. Ask the client to repeat each word after you say it. *Say _____.*
2. Use each word to complete the sentence *I see a/an _____*. Have the client repeat your sentences.
3. Print *This is a/an _____* on a card. Have the client complete the sentence using the vocabulary words.

Expressive Vocabulary
1. Name each picture.
2. What do you do at a bus stop?
3. What do you do with your bus ID card?
4. What do you do with the bus fare?
5. What does a bus driver do?
6. What does the route number tell you?
7. What information is in the bus schedule?
8. Describe the steps to boarding a bus.
9. Explain the steps to getting off at the right bus stop.
10. (Cover the pictures.) Name six city bus words.

Expressive Activity
Organize a trip using the city bus schedule. Have the client select a destination and plan which bus to board, where and when to board it, where to get off the bus, the return route, and what he needs to bring (bus ID, fare).

Critical Thinking and Problem Solving
1. How do you know what time you need to be at a city bus stop?
2. When waiting at the bus stop, what should do to make sure you're ready to board the bus?
3. What would you do if you accidentally took the wrong city bus?
4. If you think you're on the wrong city bus, what could you say to the bus driver?
5. If a passenger on a city bus is bothering you, where could you move?
6. Why should you carry your ID and phone number with you on a city bus?
7. Why should you stay awake when you ride on a city bus?
8. How do you know whether a bus that stops at your stop is the bus you want to take?
9. How can you let the bus driver know that you'd like to get off at the next stop?
10. What should you do if you miss getting off at your bus stop?

Vocabulary in the Community: Clothing Store
Functional Vocabulary for Adolescents & Adults

Clothing Store

Receptive Vocabulary
Name each picture the client points to.

1. Point to menswear (dressing room, women's department, shoe department, sportswear, outerwear).
2. Where would you find ties?
3. Which departments sells boots?
4. Where would you find blouses?
5. Which department sells workout clothes?
6. Where would you find dresses?
7. Which department sells coats?
8. Where could you try on clothes?
9. Where would you look to find clothes like the ones you're wearing?
10. Which areas of a clothing store have you been in?

Receptive Activities
Before doing these activities, make two copies of the picture grid. Cut apart one grid to make picture cards.

1. Give the client the picture grid. Have her match the picture cards to the pictures on the grid. *Where is the _____?*
2. Play a game of Bingo. Use pennies as markers.
3. Place the picture cards faceup on the table. Have the client follow your directions. *Touch the _____. Take the _____. Hand me the _____. Point to the _____. Turn over the _____.*
4. Cover three to six pictures on the picture grid. Show the client a picture card and have her tell you where it was on the picture grid. *Where was the _____?*
5. Label five blank sheets of paper with: Men's, Women's, Shoes, Outerwear, and Sportswear. Use ads from clothing stores, department stores, discount stores, or websites on the Internet. Have the clients cut out clothing pictures from each department and glue them to the correct pages. *Where would you find the _____?*
6. Visit a department store or a clothing store. Give the picture cards to the client. *Let's look for these areas in a clothing store. Find something that you would like to wear.*

Word/Sentence Imitation and Sentence Completion
1. Ask the client to repeat each word after you say it. *Say _____.*
2. Use each word to complete the sentence *I see (a/an) _____.* Have the client repeat your sentences.
3. Print *This is (a/an) _____* on a card. Have the client complete the sentence using the vocabulary words.

Expressive Vocabulary
1. Name each picture.
2. Name three stores that sell clothing.
3. Tell three items sold in each area of a clothing store.
4. Who would shop in each area of a clothing store?
5. How do you know what size the clothes are?
6. Describe a dressing room.
7. What do you do in a dressing room? Why?
8. Describe how you would shop for new pants.
9. Explain how you would shop for shoes.
10. (Cover the pictures.) Name six areas of a clothing store.

Expressive Activity
Label five blank sheets of paper with: men's, women's, shoes, outerwear, and sportswear. Look through ads from department stores, clothing stores, or the Internet. Have the clients cut out clothing pictures from each department and glue them to the correct pages. Discuss how all the items in one department go together. Ask each client to tell which clothes she would like to buy and in which department she would find each item.

Critical Thinking and Problem Solving
1. Some clothes are marked S, M, L, or XL. What do these markings mean?
2. Some pants are marked with two numbers, such as 32 x 32. What do these numbers mean?
3. What size shirt would you try on? pants? How do you decide if they fit?
4. When trying on clothes, what is important to you?
5. What kind of clothing is appropriate to wear to school?
6. What kind of clothing is appropriate to wear to work?
7. What kind of clothing is appropriate to wear when relaxing at home?
8. Why should we try to choose clothing that helps us make a good impression?
9. How does your clothing help you make an impression?
10. How do you know if your clothes at home are worn out?

Dentist's Office

Receptive Vocabulary
Name each picture the client points to.

1. Point to the dentist (X-ray, receptionist, dental floss, hygienist, cavity).
2. Who makes the appointments?
3. Who cleans your teeth?
4. Who checks the health of your teeth?
5. Which is a picture of your teeth?
6. Which is a hole in a tooth?
7. Which cleans between your teeth?
8. Which shows cavities and decay between the teeth?
9. Which do you have at home?
10. Who have you seen?

Receptive Activities
Before doing these activities, make two copies of the picture grid. Cut apart one grid to make picture cards.

1. Give the client the picture grid. Have him match the picture cards to the pictures on the grid. *Where is the _____?*
2. Play a game of Bingo. Use pennies as markers.
3. Place the picture cards faceup on the table. Have the client follow your directions. *Touch the _____. Take the _____. Hand me the _____. Point to the _____. Turn over the _____.*
4. Cover three to six pictures on the picture grid. Show the client a picture card and have him tell you where it was on the picture grid. *Where was the _____?*
5. Role-play going to a dentist. Ask the clients to wear name tags that say receptionist, hygienist, and dentist. Make pictures of X-rayed teeth, one with a cavity. Ask one client to role-play being the patient. Using the vocabulary words, give the clients directions to follow throughout the activity. *Wave to the receptionist. Sit in a chair. Open your mouth for the hygienist. Open your mouth for the dentist. Look at the X-rays. Find the tooth with the cavity.*
6. Take a tour of a dentist's office. *Let's look for (a/an) _____.*

Word/Sentence Imitation and Sentence Completion
1. Ask the client to repeat each word after you say it. *Say _____.*
2. Use each word to complete the sentence *It's (a/an) _____.* Have the client repeat your sentences.
3. Print *Here is (a/an) _____* on a card. Have the client complete the sentence using the vocabulary words.

Expressive Vocabulary
1. Name each picture.
2. What do all of these people and items have in common?
3. What does a receptionist do?
4. What does a dentist do?
5. What does a hygienist do?
6. What is the difference between a dentist and a hygienist?
7. What does an X-ray of your teeth show?
8. What happens if you get a cavity?
9. What does dental floss do?
10. (Cover the pictures.) Name three people who work at a dentist's office.

Expressive Activity
Role-play going to a dentist's office. Have the clients play the parts of the receptionist, the hygienist, the dentist, and the patient. Have each worker describe three things they do at their job. Discuss common things each person would say to a patient. Have the patient role-play meeting the receptionist and sitting in the waiting room and in the dental chair. The hygienist could pretend to take X-rays and clean the teeth. The dentist could check the X-rays, look at the patient's teeth, and make recommendations for keeping clean, healthy teeth. The receptionist could make the next appointment with the patient.

Critical Thinking and Problem Solving
1. What are some good ways to keep your teeth and mouth clean?
2. What can happen if you don't brush your teeth regularly?
3. What do you do if your tooth hurts?
4. What are three ways to have good breath?
5. Why does the dentist look at your teeth and gums?
6. Why is it important to see a dentist twice a year?
7. Why do you need to make an appointment at a dentist's office?
8. How do you make an appointment to see a dentist?
9. How can you remember when your dentist appointment is?
10. What should you do if you leave something at a dentist's office?

Discount Department Store

Receptive Vocabulary
Name each picture the client points to.

1. Point to the sports department (clothing department, electronics department, home department, toy department, garden and patio department).
2. Where would you find card games?
3. Which department has pants?
4. Where are video games located?
5. Which department has flowers?
6. Where are mixing bowls?
7. Which department has soccer balls?
8. Which department has puzzles?
9. Where would you find the clothes you are wearing?
10. Which departments have you shopped in?

Receptive Activities
Before doing these activities, make two copies of the picture grid. Cut apart one grid to make picture cards.

1. Give the client the picture grid. Have her match the picture cards to the pictures on the grid. *Where is the _____?*
2. Play a game of Bingo. Use pennies as markers.
3. Place the picture cards faceup on the table. Have the client follow your directions. *Touch the _____. Take the _____. Hand me the _____. Point to the _____. Turn over the _____.*
4. Cover three to six pictures on the picture grid. Show the client a picture card and have her tell you where it was on the picture grid. *Where was the _____?*
5. Label six blank sheets of paper with the departments in this lesson. Use ads from discount department stores (such as Target or Wal-Mart) or the Internet. Have the clients cut out pictures from each department and glue them to the correct pages. *Where would you find (a/an) _____?*
6. Visit a discount department store. Give the pictures to the client. *Let's look for these departments. Find one thing that you like in each department.*

Word/Sentence Imitation and Sentence Completion
1. Ask the client to repeat each word after you say it. *Say _____.*
2. Use each word to complete the sentence *Let's look in the _____ department.* Have the client repeat your sentences.
3. Print *I shop in the _____ department* on a card. Have the client complete the sentence using the vocabulary words.

Expressive Vocabulary
1. Name each picture.
2. Tell three things you could buy in the clothing department.
3. Name three things in the toy department.
4. Tell three things you could buy in the sports department.
5. Name three things sold in the garden and patio department.
6. Tell three things in the electronics department.
7. What is a discount department store?
8. Name a discount department store. How is it organized?
9. How is a discount department store like a grocery store? How is it different?
10. (Cover the pictures.) Name six departments in a discount store.

Expressive Activity
Look through ads from a discount department store. Label six blank sheets of paper with the departments in this lesson. Have the clients find products for each department and glue them to the correct page. Discuss what all the items in one department have in common.

Critical Thinking and Problem Solving
1. What kinds of toys are appropriate for a little girl? young boy?
2. What should you think about when buying a plant for inside your house?
3. What should you think about when buying a plant for your yard?
4. What would you do if your new clock radio doesn't work?
5. If you played soccer, what would you need to buy?
6. Why are discount department stores arranged by department?
7. How can you find out if the clothes on the rack fit you?
8. How could you get help when deciding on a blender?
9. How can you tell who the workers are at a store?
10. How do you know what department you are in?

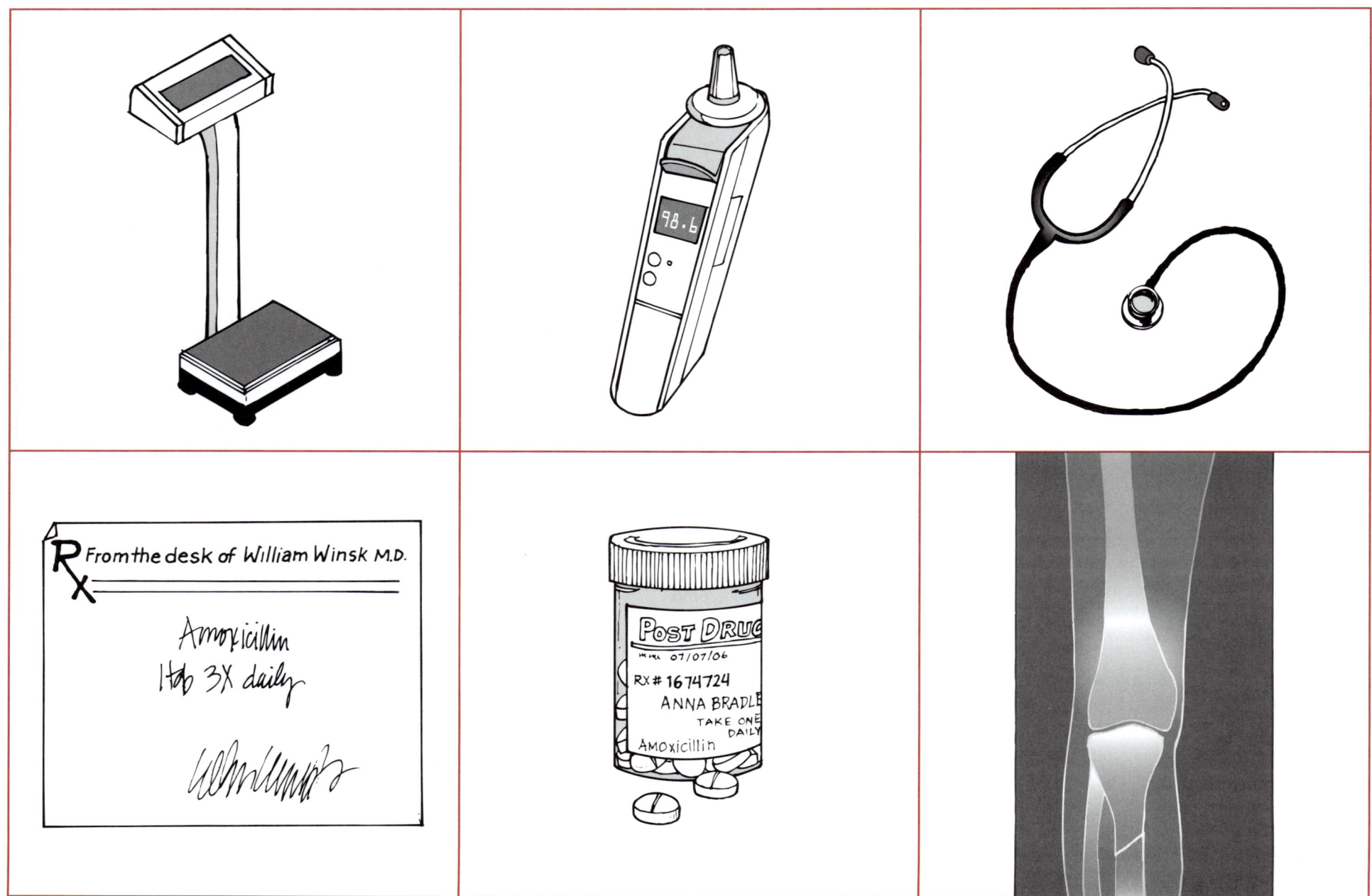

Doctor's Office

Receptive Vocabulary
Name each picture the client points to.

1. Point to the thermometer (X-ray, scale, prescription, medicine, stethoscope).
2. Which is a picture of your bones?
3. Which tells your temperature?
4. Which shows your weight?
5. Which listens to your heart?
6. Show me the paper that tells what medicine to get.
7. Which do you take when you're sick?
8. Which have numbers on them?
9. Which do you have at your house?
10. Which have you seen at a doctor's office?

Receptive Activities
Before doing these activities, make two copies of the picture grid. Cut apart one grid to make picture cards.

1. Give the client the picture grid. Have him match the picture cards to the pictures on the grid. *Where is the _____?*
2. Play a game of Bingo. Use pennies as markers.
3. Place the picture cards faceup on the table. Have the client follow your directions. *Touch the _____. Take the _____. Hand me the _____. Point to the _____. Turn over the _____.*
4. Cover three to six pictures on the picture grid. Show the client a picture card and have him tell you where it was on the picture grid. *Where was the _____?*
5. Role-play getting a checkup with a doctor. Have one client pretend to be the doctor and the other clients be the patients. Using the vocabulary words, give the clients directions to follow throughout the activity. *Stand on the scale. Use the thermometer. Use the stethoscope. Get an X-ray. Write a prescription. Buy some medicine.*
6. Take a tour of a doctor's office. *Find a/an _____.*

Word/Sentence Imitation and Sentence Completion
1. Ask the client to repeat each word after you say it. *Say _____.*
2. Use each word to complete the sentence *This is a/an _____.* Have the client repeat your sentences.
3. Print *That is a/an _____* on a card. Have the client complete the sentence using the vocabulary words.

Expressive Vocabulary
1. Name each picture.
2. What do all of these items have in common?
3. What does a scale do?
4. What does a thermometer do?
5. What does the doctor do with a stethoscope?
6. What do you do with a prescription?
7. What do you do with medicine?
8. What does an X-ray show?
9. Name three reasons you might see a doctor.
10. (Cover the pictures.) Name six items you'd see at a doctor's office.

Expressive Activity
Role-play getting a checkup with a doctor. Have one client pretend to be the doctor and the other client pretend to be the patient. Have the doctor explain what he is doing as he uses the scale, thermometer, stethoscope, and X-ray machine, and while he is writing the prescription. Then let different clients pretend to be the doctor.

Critical Thinking and Problem Solving
1. What do you feel like when you have a fever?
2. If you have a fever, what kind of medicine could you take?
3. If you have a runny nose, what kind of medicine could you take?
4. If you have a cough, what kind of medicine could you take?
5. What could happen if you take too much medicine?
6. What should you do if you think you broke a bone?
7. How are medicines different?
8. How can you find out if you have a fever?
9. How do you know how much medicine to take and how often to take it?
10. How do you decide whether to make a doctor's appointment or go to the emergency room?

Fast-Food Restaurant

Receptive Vocabulary
Name each picture the client points to.

1. Point to the cashier (trash, tray, booth, menu, beverage).
2. Which lists the food choices?
3. Which shows the prices?
4. Who takes your order?
5. Who do you pay?
6. Which do you use to carry your food to a table?
7. Which do you drink?
8. Where do you sit?
9. Where do you throw away garbage?
10. Which have you seen at a fast-food restaurant?

Receptive Activities
Before doing these activities, make two copies of the picture grid. Cut apart one grid to make picture cards.

1. Give the client the picture grid. Have her match the picture cards to the pictures on the grid. *Where is the _____?*
2. Place the picture cards faceup on the table. Have the client follow your directions. *Touch the _____. Take the _____. Hand me the _____. Point to the _____. Turn over the _____.*
3. Cover three to six pictures on the picture grid. Show the client a picture card and have her tell you where it was on the picture grid. *Where was the _____?*
4. Role-play going to a fast-food restaurant. Have clients use a picture menu and pretend to order a meal. (McDonald's gives menus out; other fast-food restaurants have pictures of menu items on the Internet.) Use trays, cups, and paper sacks for the food service, and line chairs along tables like a booth. Ask one client to be the cashier and the other clients to be the customers. Using the vocabulary words, give the clients directions to follow throughout the activity. *Find the cashier. Show her your menu. Show her a beverage on your menu. Get the tray. Take it to the booth.*
5. Visit a fast-food restaurant. Give the pictures to the client. *Let's look for a/the _____.*

Word/Sentence Imitation and Sentence Completion
1. Ask the client to repeat each word after you say it. *Say _____.*
2. Use each word to complete the sentence *I see a _____.* Have the client repeat your sentences.
3. Print *Here is a _____* on a card. Have the client complete the sentence using the vocabulary words.

Expressive Vocabulary
1. Name each picture.
2. What does this person and all of these items have in common?
3. What is on a menu?
4. What does the cashier do?
5. What do you do with a tray?
6. Name three beverages you might see.
7. Describe a booth.
8. What do you do with your paper goods when you're finished eating?
9. Name three fast-food restaurants.
10. (Cover the pictures.) Name six items and people you'd see at a fast-food restaurant.

Expressive Activity
Role-play going to a fast-food restaurant. One client can pretend to be the cashier, and the other clients can pretend to be the customers. Write menu items on the board, and use a calculator for a cash register. Use trays, cups, and paper sacks to mimic the food service, and line chairs along tables like a booth. Have the clients practice ordering food, paying, getting the tray, filling the drink at the soda machine, and sitting at a booth with friends. Ask the clients to describe what they are doing throughout the activity.

Critical Thinking and Problem Solving
1. What could you do if you don't have enough money to order what you want?
2. What if the beverage machine is out of the drink you want?
3. What are some good manners to use while eating at a fast-food restaurant?
4. What could you talk about while eating with your friends?
5. What should you do if the cashier gives you the wrong order?
6. When do you use the drive-through instead of going inside the restaurant?
7. When would you go to a fast-food restaurant instead of a restaurant?
8. Why is it important to read the prices before ordering?
9. Why should you sit at the same table as your friends?
10. How do you decide if your food order is for "here" or "to go"?

Grocery Shopping

Receptive Vocabulary
Name each picture the client points to.

1. Point to the receipt (shopping cart, checkout line, grocery list, cashier, cash register).
2. Which paper shows what you want to buy?
3. Which do you put groceries in?
4. Which has wheels?
5. Where do you pay for your groceries?
6. Which adds prices?
7. Who takes your money?
8. Who gives you change?
9. Which paper shows what you bought?
10. Which paper shows the prices of what you bought?

Receptive Activities
Before doing these activities, make two copies of the picture grid. Cut apart one grid to make picture cards.

1. Give the client the picture grid. Have him match the picture cards to the pictures on the grid. *Where is the _____?*
2. Play a game of Bingo. Use pennies as markers.
3. Place the picture cards faceup on the table. Have the client follow your directions. *Touch the _____. Take the _____. Hand me the _____. Point to the _____. Turn over the _____.*
4. Cover three to six pictures on the picture grid. Show the client a picture card and have him tell you where it was on the picture grid. *Where was the _____?*
5. Role-play grocery shopping. Have one client be the cashier and the other clients be the customers. Make a shopping list, have a few products (or empty containers) that they can purchase, use a calculator as a cash register, and have some grocery bags. Using the vocabulary words, give the clients directions to follow throughout the activity. *Bring your grocery list. Pretend to push your shopping cart. Get your groceries. Get in the checkout line. Pay the cashier.*
6. Visit a grocery store. Give the pictures to the client. *Let's look for a _____.*

Word/Sentence Imitation and Sentence Completion
1. Ask the client to repeat each word after you say it. *Say _____.*
2. Use each word to complete the sentence *Here is a _____.* Have the client repeat your sentences.
3. Print *This is a _____* on a card. Have the client complete the sentence using the vocabulary words.

Expressive Vocabulary
1. Name each picture.
2. What do you do with each item?
3. What does this person and all of these items have in common?
4. Name three things that could be on a shopping list.
5. What do you do at the checkout line?
6. What is the difference between a grocery list and a receipt?
7. Tell three things a cashier does.
8. Describe what a cash register looks like and what it does.
9. What information is on a receipt?
10. (Cover the pictures.) Name six items and people you'd see while grocery shopping.

Expressive Activity
Role-play grocery shopping. Have one client be the cashier and the other clients be the customers. Discuss what they will need. Have one client make a shopping list and another client gather items (real, empty, or made containers) they could purchase at a grocery store. Create a cash register using a calculator, and arrange a table to look like a checkout line with grocery bags at the end. Have the customers discuss the steps to shopping and the cashier talk about what he does.

Critical Thinking and Problem Solving
1. How do you know what to put on a grocery list?
2. How do you decide if you are going to use a shopping cart or a basket?
3. Why should you be careful when pushing a shopping cart?
4. How do you know what size of each item to buy?
5. How do you decide which brands to buy?
6. How can you calculate your total cost before you reach the cashier?
7. What do you do if you don't have enough money to buy all of your groceries?
8. What greeting could you say to the cashier?
9. How can you calculate if the cashier gave you the correct change back?
10. How can you tell who works at the store and who is a customer?

Grocery Store

Receptive Vocabulary
Name each picture the client points to.

1. Point to dairy (produce, canned foods, bakery, frozen foods, meat).
2. Where would you find apples?
3. Which section has hamburger?
4. Where is the canned tuna?
5. Which section has fresh bread?
6. Which section has frozen vegetables?
7. Which section has milk?
8. Which section has bananas?
9. Which sections are cold?
10. Which sections have you shopped in?

Receptive Activities
Before doing these activities, make two copies of the picture grid. Cut apart one grid to make picture cards.

1. Give the client the picture grid. Have her match the picture cards to the pictures on the grid. *Where is the _____?*
2. Play a game of Bingo. Use pennies as markers.
3. Place the picture cards faceup on the table. Have the client follow your directions. *Touch the _____. Take the _____. Hand me the _____. Point to the _____. Turn over the _____.*
4. Cover three to six pictures on the picture grid. Show the client a picture card and have her tell you where it was on the picture grid. *Where was the _____?*
5. Label six blank sheets of paper with the vocabulary words. Cut out pictures of different foods from food magazines or grocery store ads. Have the client glue each food to the correct page. *Where would you find (a/an) _____?*
6. Visit a grocery store. Give the pictures to the client. *Let's look for the _____ section. Find three foods you like in each section.*

Word/Sentence Imitation and Sentence Completion
1. Ask the client to repeat each word after you say it. *Say _____.*
2. Use each word to complete the sentence *Let's go to the _____ section.* Have the client repeat your sentences.
3. Print *I see the _____ section* on a card. Have the client complete the sentence using the vocabulary words.

Expressive Vocabulary
1. Name each picture.
2. Name three items you could buy in each section.
3. What do produce items have in common?
4. How are dairy items similar?
5. What do meat products have in common?
6. How are bakery items similar?
7. Describe a frozen foods section.
8. How are canned foods similar?
9. Tell how your grocery store is organized.
10. (Cover the pictures.) Name six sections in a grocery store.

Expressive Activity
Label six blank sheets of paper with the vocabulary words. Then cut out pictures of different foods from magazines or grocery store ads. Have the client talk about which section of a grocery store each item would be found in before gluing it to the corresponding sheet of paper. When the pages are finished, ask her to discuss how all the items in one section are the same.

Critical Thinking and Problem Solving
1. What does the date mean on milk containers? meat packages?
2. What do you do with food in your refrigerator that has an old date on it?
3. What would you do if you accidentally knocked over some boxes in a grocery store?
4. What would you do if one of your packages leaked in your shopping cart?
5. What would happen if you put ice cream in your shopping cart at the beginning of your shopping trip?
6. Why is it a good idea to get your frozen foods last?
7. How do you choose which bananas to buy? oranges? tomatoes?
8. How can you tell if the fruits or vegetables in your refrigerator are old?
9. How can you tell how many servings are in a can of food?
10. How could you order a cake?

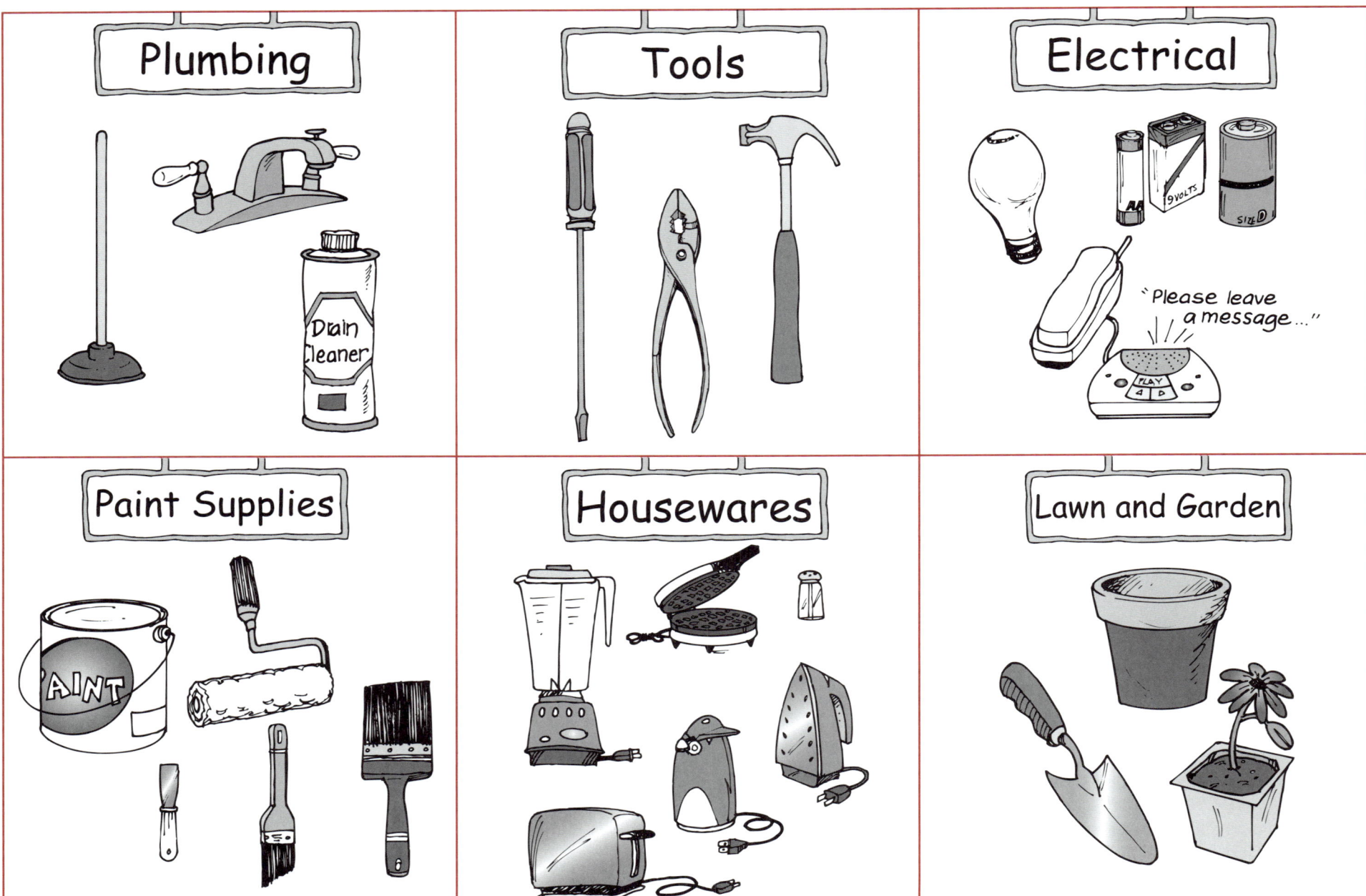

Hardware Store

Receptive Vocabulary
Name each picture the client points to.

1. Point to the paint supplies department (tool department, housewares department, plumbing department, lawn and garden department, electrical department).
2. Where would you find batteries?
3. Where would you find paint?
4. Where would you find a hammer?
5. Where would you find a faucet?
6. Where would you find a flower basket?
7. Where would you find a blender?
8. Which are departments at a hardware store?
9. Which departments have items for your home?
10. Which departments have you been in?

Receptive Activities
Before doing these activities, make two copies of the picture grid. Cut apart one grid to make picture cards.

1. Give the client the picture grid. Have him match the picture cards to the pictures on the grid. *Where is the _____?*
2. Play a game of Bingo. Use pennies as markers.
3. Place the picture cards faceup on the table. Have the client follow your directions. *Touch the _____. Take the _____. Hand me the _____. Point to the _____. Turn over the _____.*
4. Cover three to six pictures on the picture grid. Show the client a picture card and have him tell you where it was on the picture grid. *Where was the _____?*
5. Label six blank sheets of paper with the vocabulary words. Use ads from a hardware store or look on hardware store websites. Cut out items that would be sold in each department of the store and have the client glue them to the correct page. *Where would you find (a/an) _____?*
6. Visit a hardware store. Give the pictures to the client. *Let's look for the _____ department.*

Word/Sentence Imitation and Sentence Completion
1. Ask the client to repeat each word after you say it. *Say _____.*
2. Use each word to complete the sentence *Look in the _____ department.* Have the client repeat your sentences.
3. Print *The _____ department is here* on a card. Have the client complete the sentence using the vocabulary words.

Expressive Vocabulary
1. Name each section of a hardware store.
2. Name three things sold in each department.
3. What do plumbing items have in common?
4. What do tools have in common?
5. How are electrical supplies the same?
6. What do paint supplies have in common?
7. How are items in the housewares department the same?
8. What do the lawn and garden supplies have in common?
9. Describe how a hardware store is organized.
10. (Cover the pictures.) Name six items you could find in a hardware store.

Expressive Activity
Label six blank sheets of paper with the vocabulary words. Then cut out pictures of different items you can buy in a hardware store. Have the client talk about which section of a hardware store each item would be found in before gluing it to the corresponding sheet of paper. Discuss how all the items in one department go together.

Critical Thinking and Problem Solving
1. What are some good safety rules for using a kitchen knife?
2. What is a good safety rule for using a hammer?
3. What are two kinds of screwdrivers? How do you know which one to use?
4. When gardening, when would you use a trowel instead of a shovel?
5. How do you know when you need a new light bulb?
6. Why is it a good idea to turn off a lamp before changing the light bulb?
7. Why is it a good idea to put a drop cloth down before painting a wall?
8. How can you clean a paintbrush after painting?
9. Why are hardware stores arranged by departments?
10. How do you know what department of a hardware store you are in?

Vocabulary in the Community: Library/Bookstore

Library/Bookstore

Receptive Vocabulary
Name each picture the client points to.

1. Point to the magazines (reference books, novels, paperback books, videos/DVDs, children's books).
2. Which are movies?
3. Which have stories?
4. Which have facts?
5. Which have soft covers?
6. Which has articles?
7. Which can be mailed monthly?
8. Which have pictures?
9. Which have you seen?
10. Which do you like?

Receptive Activities
Before doing these activities, make two copies of the picture grid. Cut apart one grid to make picture cards.

1. Give the client the picture grid. Have him match the picture cards to the pictures on the grid. *Where are the _____?*
2. Place a magazine, paperback book, reference book, video, DVD, children's book, and adult book on the table. Give a picture card to the client. *Find the _____.*
3. Place the picture cards faceup on the table. Have the client follow your directions. *Touch the _____. Take the _____. Hand me the _____. Point to the _____. Turn over the _____.*
4. Use these pictures for a scavenger hunt. Have the clients look for items in your classroom or school. *Find a _____.*
5. Look up websites that sell books, magazines, videos, and DVDs. Print out the pictures and have the client glue them to a poster titled: Library / Bookstore. Then ask the client to identify the different items on the poster. *Find a _____.*
6. Visit a library or a bookstore. Use the pictures to find the different sections in the library or bookstore. *Let's look for the _____.*

Word/Sentence Imitation and Sentence Completion
1. Ask the client to repeat each word after you say it. *Say _____.*
2. Use each word to complete the sentence *I read _____.* Have the client repeat your sentences.
3. Print *Look in the _____ section* on a card. Have the client complete the sentence using the vocabulary words.

Expressive Vocabulary
1. Name each picture.
2. What do all of these items have in common?
3. Describe a magazine.
4. How is a paperback book different from a hardback book?
5. Name three reference books.
6. How are children's books different from adult novels?
7. Name three videos or DVDs.
8. What do you like to read?
9. What is the difference between a library and a bookstore?
10. (Cover the pictures.) Name six items you'd find in a library or bookstore.

Expressive Activity
Plan a trip to a library or a bookstore. Have the client make a list of what he would like to look at while there. Talk about which section he could look in to find each item.

Critical Thinking and Problem Solving
1. Why is it a good idea to be quiet in a library?
2. Why is it a good idea to return your library book on time?
3. How could you make a plan to visit a library or a bookstore with a friend?
4. How are the books organized in your library? bookstore?
5. How are the videos organized in your library? How do you find the video or DVD you like?
6. How are the magazines organized in the bookstore? How do you find a magazine you like?
7. How can you tell if a book is easy to read or hard to read?
8. How can you tell if a book is going to be scary? funny?
9. What can you do if you can't find a book you like?
10. How do you decide if you will like a book?

Pet Store

Receptive Vocabulary
Name each picture the client points to.

1. Point to the cat food (fish tank, turtle, leash, hamster, birdcage).
2. Which would you buy for a dog?
3. Which is for fish?
4. Which is for a cat?
5. Which is for a bird?
6. Which has a shell?
7. Which has fur?
8. Which are animals?
9. Which hold animals?
10. Which do you have at your home?

Receptive Activities
Before doing these activities, make two copies of the picture grid. Cut apart one grid to make picture cards.

1. Give the client the picture grid. Have him match the picture cards to the pictures on the grid. *Where is the _____?*
2. Play a game of Bingo. Use pennies as markers.
3. Place the picture cards faceup on the table. Have the client follow your directions. *Touch the _____. Take the _____. Hand me the _____. Point to the _____. Turn over the _____.*
4. Cover three to six pictures on the picture grid. Show the client a picture card and have him tell you where it was on the picture grid. *Where was the _____?*
5. Use ads from a pet store or a website that contains pet supplies. *Find (a) _____.*
6. Visit a local pet store. Give the picture cards to the client. *Let's look for (a) _____.*

Word/Sentence Imitation and Sentence Completion
1. Ask the client to repeat each word after you say it. *Say _____.*
2. Use each word to complete the sentence *That's (a) _____.* Have the client repeat your sentences.
3. Print *Let's buy (a) _____* on a card. Have the client complete the sentence using the vocabulary words.

Expressive Vocabulary
1. Name each picture.
2. What do all of these animals and items have in common?
3. What do you do with a leash?
4. What is the difference between canned and dry cat food?
5. Tell what animals can live in a birdcage.
6. Describe what animals can live in a fish tank.
7. Where would you keep a hamster?
8. Where would you keep a turtle?
9. Do you have any pets? If so, what kind?
10. (Cover the pictures.) Name six items or animals you could see at a pet store.

Expressive Activity
Have two students role-play going to a pet store to buy a pet. One client can be the customer, and the other client can be the store clerk. Have the clients discuss the different pets and what type of supplies and care each pet requires.

Critical Thinking and Problem Solving
1. What could happen if you stuck your finger into a bird's cage?
2. What could happen if you pet a strange dog?
3. What do cat owners do to take care of their cats?
4. What do dog owners do to take care of their dogs?
5. If you could buy a new pet, what would it be? How would you take care of it?
6. How do you decide which kind of pet food to buy?
7. How do you decide which kind of cage to buy?
8. What do you do if you can't find something in a pet store? How do you know who a worker is?
9. What if a pet gets sick?
10. What happens when a pet owner wants to go on vacation?

Vocabulary in the Community: Restaurant

Restaurant

Receptive Vocabulary
Name each picture the client points to.

1. Point to the menu (beverage, check, appetizer, tip, dessert).
2. Which lists the food choices?
3. Which gives the food prices?
4. Which do you eat first?
5. Which do you drink?
6. Which treat comes at the end of a meal?
7. Which tells how much money you owe?
8. Which do you leave for the server?
9. Which of these can you eat?
10. Which have you seen at a restaurant?

Receptive Activities
Before doing these activities, make two copies of the picture grid. Cut apart one grid to make picture cards.

1. Give the client the picture grid. Have her match the picture cards to the pictures on the grid. *Where is the _____?*
2. Place the picture cards faceup on the table. Have the client follow your directions. *Touch the _____. Take the _____. Hand me the _____. Point to the _____. Turn over the _____.*
3. Cover three to six pictures on the picture grid. Show the client a picture card and have her tell you where it was on the picture grid. *Where was the _____?*
4. Role-play going to a restaurant. Use borrowed menus from a local restaurant, dishes, pretend money, and a mock check. Have one client play the server and the other clients be the customers. Ask the customers to sit around a table and the server to hand out menus. Using the vocabulary words, give the clients directions to follow throughout the activity. *Look at the menus. To order, point to a beverage.* Have the server bring out dishes (with or without food/drinks) and later the check, and give additional directions. *Look at the check. Pay for your food. Leave a tip.*
5. Visit a restaurant. Give the picture cards to the client. *Let's look for a _____.*

Word/Sentence Imitation and Sentence Completion
1. Ask the client to repeat each word after you say it. *Say _____.*
2. Use each word to complete the sentence *This is a/an _____.* Have the client repeat your sentences.
3. Print *I see a/an _____* on a card. Have the client complete the sentence using the vocabulary words.

Expressive Vocabulary
1. Name each picture.
2. What is on a menu?
3. Name three appetizers.
4. Name three beverages.
5. Name three desserts.
6. What is on the bill?
7. What is the tip for?
8. Name three restaurants.
9. How are restaurants different from eating at home?
10. (Cover the pictures.) Name six items you'd see at a restaurant.

Expressive Activity
Have your clients role-play going to a restaurant. One client can pretend to be the host/hostess, another client can be the server, and the other clients can pretend to be the customers. Have them practice meeting the host/hostess and telling the number of people in their group, going to the table and reading the menu, ordering, being served, paying, and leaving a tip. For added challenge, have the server make mistakes, such as forgetting silverware, bringing the wrong order, or not bringing the drinks. Help them problem solve what to ask the server to correct the mistakes.

Critical Thinking and Problem Solving
1. What if there aren't enough glasses of water on the table?
2. What if you drop your spoon?
3. What are some good table manners to use while eating at the restaurant?
4. What information do you give a hostess when you first enter a restaurant?
5. When would you go to a restaurant instead of a fast-food restaurant?
6. Why should you look at the food prices before ordering?
7. How do you make a reservation? How can you find the phone number?
8. How do you decide whether or not to order appetizers?
9. How do you know if you have enough money for dessert?
10. How do you calculate the tip?

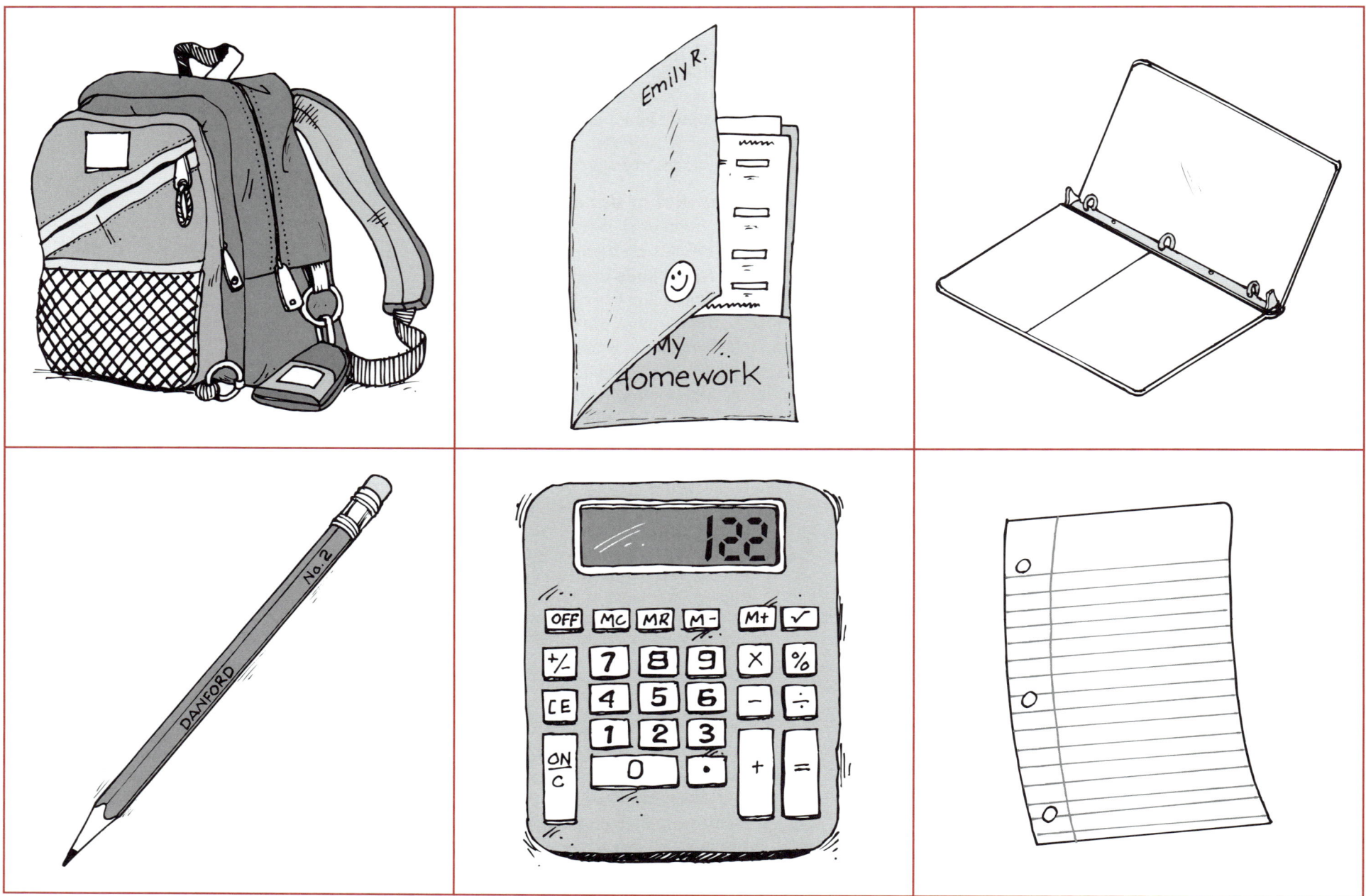

School Supplies

Receptive Vocabulary
Name each picture the client points to.

1. Point to the backpack (paper, folder, calculator, binder, pencil).
2. Which can you carry on your back?
3. Which adds numbers?
4. Which do you write with?
5. Which can you write on?
6. Which can you put papers in?
7. Which has a zipper?
8. Which has buttons?
9. Which has an eraser?
10. Which do you use at school?

Receptive Activities
Before doing these activities, make two copies of the picture grid. Cut apart one grid to make picture cards.

1. Give the client the picture grid. Have him match the picture cards to the pictures on the grid. *Where is the _____?*
2. Place a real backpack, folder, etc. on the table. Give a picture card to the client and have him put it by the matching item. *Find the _____.*
3. Ask the clients to look through their backpacks (or a backpack you provide). *Find the _____.*
4. Place picture cards faceup on the table. Have the client follow your directions. *Touch the _____. Take the _____. Hand me the _____. Point to the _____. Turn over the _____.*
5. Cover three to six pictures on the picture grid. Show the client a picture card and have him tell you where it was on the picture grid. *Where was the _____?*
6. Use ads from a discount store, an office supply store, or the Internet. *Find (a) _____.*
7. Visit a discount store or an office supply store. Use the pictures as a shopping list. *Let's look for (a) _____.*

Word/Sentence Imitation and Sentence Completion
1. Ask the client to repeat each word after you say it. *Say _____.*
2. Use each word to complete the sentence *I use (a) _____.* Have the client repeat your sentences.
3. Print *I have (a) _____* on a card. Have the client complete the sentence using the vocabulary words.

Expressive Vocabulary
1. Name each picture.
2. What do all of these items have in common?
3. Which do you have?
4. What do yours look like?
5. What do you do with each item?
6. Where do you keep each item?
7. When do you use each item?
8. What else can you write with?
9. Describe how you organize your school supplies.
10. (Cover the pictures.) What six items should you bring to school?

Expressive Activity
Have your clients role-play helping a new student. Have one client pretend to be a new student, and the others can be the veterans. Have the veterans explain to the new student what they bring to school each day, how they use each item, and why each item is important.

Critical Thinking and Problem Solving
1. What if you break your pencil lead?
2. What if your backpack zipper gets stuck?
3. What if your lunch spills in your backpack?
4. What if your calculator stops working?
5. What if your binder gets filled with too many papers?
6. What would a teacher think if your papers were crumpled?
7. How do you keep track of your homework?
8. What if you forgot to write down your homework assignment?
9. What is a good way to organize your backpack?
10. What is a good way to organize your binder?

Signs

Receptive Vocabulary
Name each picture the client points to.

1. Point to walk (don't walk, do not enter, stop, exit, caution).
2. Which means "Do not cross the street"?
3. Which means "Yes, cross the street"?
4. Which means "Halt"?
5. Which means "This way outside"?
6. Which means "Do not go in"?
7. Which means "Be careful"?
8. Which do you see at an intersection?
9. Which do you see in buildings?
10. Which mean "Don't go there"?

Receptive Activities
Before doing these activities, make two copies of the picture grid. Cut apart one grid to make picture cards.

1. Give the client the picture grid. Have her match the picture cards to the pictures on the grid. *Where is _____?*
2. Play a game of Bingo. Use pennies as markers.
3. Place picture cards faceup on the table. Have the client follow your directions. *Touch _____. Take _____. Hand me _____. Point to _____. Turn over _____.*
4. Cover three to six pictures on the picture grid. Show the client a picture card and have her tell you where it was on the picture grid. *Where was _____?*
5. Go for a walk that includes an intersection with a stoplight and an intersection with a stop sign. Give the pictures to the student. *Let's look for _____.*
6. Visit a hardware store. Look at various signs that can be purchased. *Let's look for Do Not Enter, Exit, and Caution.*

Word/Sentence Imitation and Sentence Completion
1. Ask the client to repeat each word after you say it. *Say _____.*
2. Use each word to complete the sentence *This means _____.* Have the client repeat your sentences.
3. Print *This sign means _____* on a card. Have the client complete the sentence using the vocabulary words.

Expressive Vocabulary
1. Name each picture.
2. What does each sign mean?
3. Where have you seen each sign?
4. Which have you seen today?
5. What are some other traffic signs?
6. What other signs are at a school?
7. What signs would you see at a construction site?
8. Name three places you'd see a caution sign.
9. Describe how to cross a street safely.
10. (Cover the pictures.) Name six signs.

Expressive Activity
Go for a walk that includes crossing a street at a street light and at an intersection with a stop sign. Talk about how those signs help you to cross the street safely.

Critical Thinking and Problem Solving
1. If a crosswalk shows the walk signal, do you still need to look for cars? Why?
2. If a crosswalk shows the walk signal and a car is coming, what should you do? Why?
3. If a crosswalk shows the walk signal and a car is stopped, is it okay to cross the street? Why?
4. If a crosswalk starts blinking the don't walk signal when you're only halfway across the street, what should you do? Why?
5. If a sign outside a rest room door says "Do Not Enter," should you open the door?
6. If there's a caution sign next to a river, should you swim in the river?
7. If a machine has a caution sign on it, should you touch the machine?
8. How do you know which door leads to the outside?
9. Why do people post signs?
10. Why should you read signs?

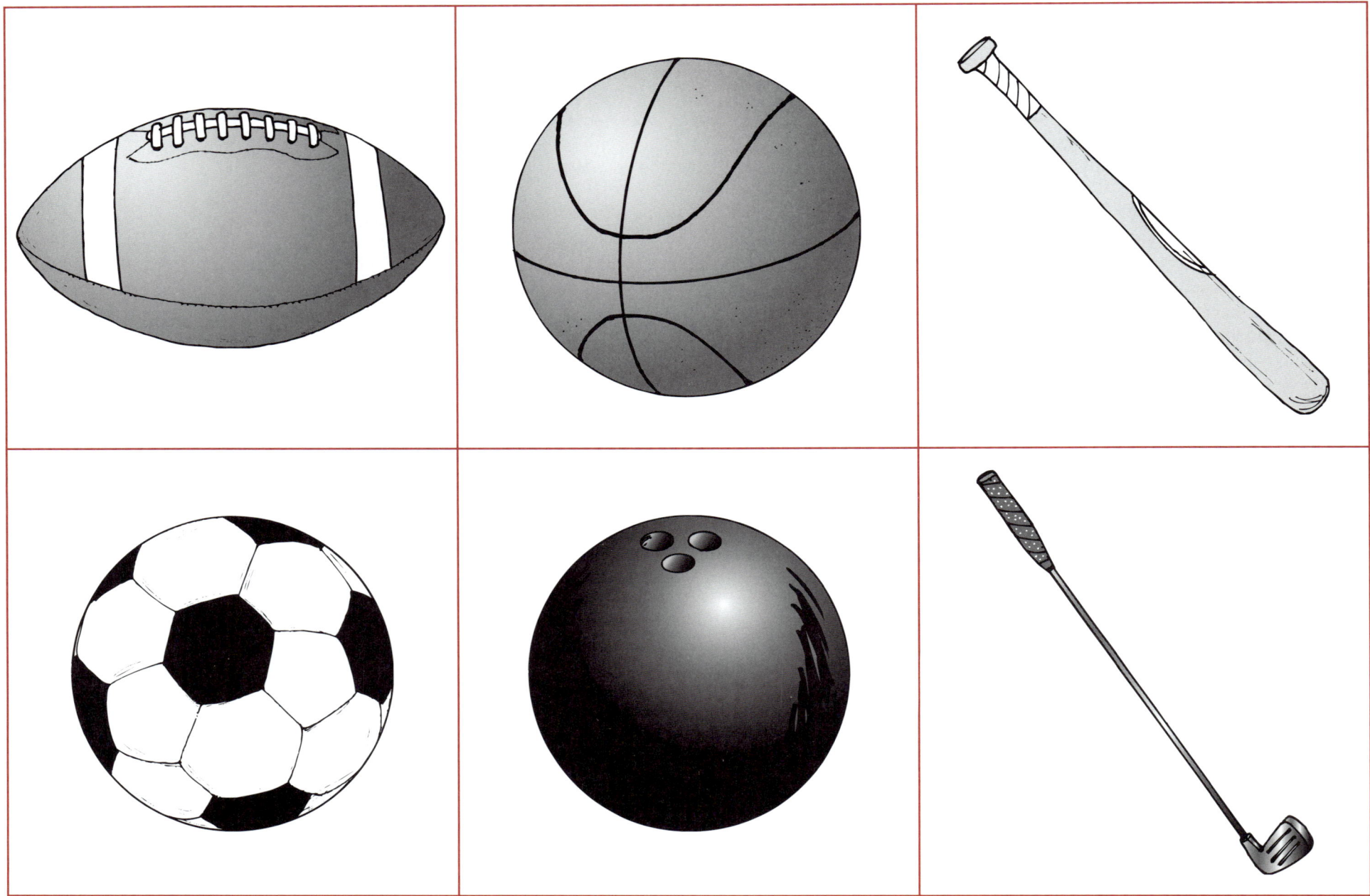

Vocabulary in the Community: Sporting Goods Store
Functional Vocabulary for Adolescents & Adults

Sporting Goods Store

Receptive Vocabulary
Name each picture the client points to.

1. Point to the football (baseball bat, bowling ball, basketball, golf club, soccer ball).
2. Which are balls?
3. Which can you kick?
4. Which do you throw in a hoop?
5. Which goes with a baseball?
6. Which goes with a golf ball?
7. Which goes with bowling pins?
8. Which do you use to make a touchdown?
9. Which have you used?
10. Which do you like?

Receptive Activities
Before doing these activities, make two copies of the picture grid. Cut apart one grid to make picture cards.

1. Give the client the picture grid. Have him match the picture cards to the pictures on the grid. *Where is the _____?*
2. Place a real football, basketball, etc., on the table. Give a picture card to the client and have him put it by the matching item. *Find the _____.*
3. Play a pantomime game using the picture cards or real items. *Show me how you use this.*
4. Place the picture cards faceup on the table. Have the client follow your directions. *Touch the _____. Take the _____. Hand me the _____. Point to the _____. Turn over the _____.*
5. Cover three to six pictures on the picture grid. Show the client a picture card and have him tell you where it was on the picture grid. *Where was the _____?*
6. Use ads or websites from a sporting goods store. Cut out pictures and glue them to a poster titled Sporting Goods. *Find (a/an) _____.*
7. Visit a sporting goods store. Give the pictures to the student. *Let's look for a _____.*

Word/Sentence Imitation and Sentence Completion
1. Ask the client to repeat each word after you say it. *Say _____.*
2. Use each word to complete the sentence *I use a _____.* Have the client repeat your sentences.
3. Print *Grab the _____* on a card. Have the client complete the sentence using the vocabulary words.

Expressive Vocabulary
1. Name each picture.
2. What do all of these items have in common?
3. What do you do with each item?
4. Tell what sport you could play with each item.
5. Where could you buy each item?
6. Name a sporting goods store.
7. What sports have you played?
8. Which sports are your favorites? Why?
9. Describe how to bowl.
10. (Cover the pictures.) Name six sports items.

Expressive Activity
Talk about the different sports played in PE. Write the name of each sport at the top of a sheet of construction paper. Have the clients look through ads from a sporting goods store and cut out pictures of various sports equipment. Have them glue each picture on the appropriate sheet and talk about how each item is used in the sport.

Critical Thinking and Problem Solving
1. What do you need to play football? Where could you play?
2. What do you need to play basketball? Where could you play?
3. What do you need to play baseball? Where could you play?
4. What do you need to play soccer? Where could you play?
5. What do you need to bowl? Where could you bowl?
6. What do you need to golf? Where could you golf?
7. What if your ball is flat?
8. How do you know which way to run in a game?
9. How does a good sport act when she loses? when she wins?
10. Why is it important to be a good sport?

Stationery Store

Receptive Vocabulary
Name each picture the client points to.

1. Point to a wedding card (congratulations card, birthday card, get-well card, invitation, thank-you card).
2. What do all of these items have in common?
3. Which is for a birthday?
4. Which is for a bride and groom?
5. Which is for a graduate?
6. Which is for someone who's sick?
7. Which invites people to a party?
8. Which is to thank someone?
9. Which have you received?
10. Which have you sent?

Receptive Activities
Before doing these activities, make two copies of the picture grid. Cut apart one grid to make picture cards.

1. Give the client the picture grid. Have her match the picture cards to the pictures on the grid. *Where is the _____?*
2. Play a game of Bingo. Use pennies as markers.
3. Place real cards for various occasions on the table. Give a picture card to the client and have her put it by the matching item. *Find the _____.*
4. Place the picture cards faceup on the table. Have the client follow your directions. *Touch the _____. Take the _____. Hand me the _____. Point to the _____. Turn over the _____.*
5. Cover three to six pictures on the picture grid. Show the client a picture card and have her tell you where it was on the picture grid. *Where was the _____?*
6. Use an Internet search engine to find a website that contains greeting cards. *Find a/an _____.*
7. Visit a store that sells cards. Use the pictures as a shopping list. *Let's look for a/an _____.*

Word/Sentence Imitation and Sentence Completion
1. Ask the client to repeat each word after you say it. *Say _____.*
2. Use each word to complete the sentence *I'll buy a/an _____.* Have the client repeat your sentences.
3. Print *I'll send a/an _____* on a card. Have the client complete the sentence using the vocabulary words.

Expressive Vocabulary
1. Name each picture.
2. What do all of these items have in common?
3. What is on an invitation?
4. Who could you give birthday cards to?
5. When do people send get-well cards?
6. Who receives wedding cards?
7. Name three reasons you could send thank-you cards.
8. Tell three things people could be congratulated for.
9. Name three places that sell cards.
10. (Cover the pictures.) Name six kinds of cards.

Expressive Activity
Have the client look through a calendar. Talk about different holidays and special events and which cards she could send or give at those times.

Critical Thinking and Problem Solving
1. What do you think about when buying a birthday card for someone?
2. What do you think about when buying a get-well card for someone?
3. What is the difference between a wedding card and an anniversary card?
4. What information should you include in a thank-you card?
5. What card could you buy someone who is graduating?
6. Which would you buy for a couple getting married?
7. When sending invitations, what information should you include on your card?
8. When you get an invitation, what information can you put on your calendar?
9. Why is it a good idea to RSVP when you get an invitation?
10. How do you think others feel when they receive a card?

Vocabulary in the Community: Toy Store

Toy Store

Receptive Vocabulary
Name each picture the client points to.

1. Point to the stuffed animals (puzzles, sporting goods, board games, video games, arts and crafts).
2. Which are furry?
3. Which has controllers?
4. Which is for ballgames?
5. Which have dice?
6. Which make a picture?
7. Which get put together?
8. Which do you play with outside?
9. Which do you play with inside?
10. Which do you like?

Receptive Activities
Before doing these activities, make two copies of the picture grid. Cut apart one grid to make picture cards.

1. Give the client the picture grid. Have him match the picture cards to the pictures on the grid. *Where is the _____?*
2. Play a game of Bingo. Use pennies as markers.
3. Place the picture cards faceup on the table. Have the client follow your directions. *Touch the _____. Take the _____. Hand me the _____. Point to the _____. Turn over the _____.*
4. Cover three to six pictures on the picture grid. Show the client a picture card and have him tell you where it was on the picture grid. *Where were the _____?*
5. Look at ads or websites for a toy store. Cut out pictures of items and glue them to a poster labeled Toy Store. *Find (a/an) _____.*
6. Visit a toy store. Give the client the picture cards. *Let's find the _____.*

Word/Sentence Imitation and Sentence Completion
1. Ask the client to repeat each word after you say it. *Say _____.*
2. Use each word to complete the sentence *Let's look for the _____.* Have the client repeat your sentences.
3. Print *Let's buy some _____* on a card. Have the client complete the sentence using the vocabulary words.

Expressive Vocabulary
1. Name each picture.
2. What do all of these items have in common?
3. Describe a board game.
4. Tell what you do with a puzzle.
5. Explain how you play video games.
6. Name three arts and crafts supplies.
7. Name three types of sport equipment.
8. Describe three different kinds of stuffed animals.
9. What toys could you buy a young friend?
10. (Cover the pictures.) Name six items you'd find at a toy store.

Expressive Activity
Label six blank sheets of paper Board Games, Puzzles, Video Games, Arts & Crafts, Sporting Goods, and Stuffed Animals. Look through ads or websites for toy stores. Have the clients cut out pictures of three items from each category and glue them to the correct page. Discuss how all the items in one section go together. Talk about what they would like to purchase and where they would find it in a toy store.

Critical Thinking and Problem Solving
1. What useful information is on the board game box?
2. What do you consider when choosing a puzzle?
3. What do you consider when choosing a video game?
4. What if you can't find the stuffed animals in the toy store?
5. What if you can't reach a toy on the top shelf?
6. What if the price is not marked on the toy you'd like to buy?
7. If your friend likes arts and crafts, what would be some good gift ideas?
8. If your friend likes sports, what would be some good gift ideas?
9. Why is it a good idea to consider what your friend likes when buying her a gift?
10. Why is it a good idea to look at the price before buying an item?

Job Choices

Receptive Vocabulary
Name each picture the client points to.

1. Point to the garden workers (housecleaners, restaurant workers, office helpers, laundry workers, and store employees).
2. Who washes laundry?
3. Who works with papers and files?
4. Who puts new products on a shelf?
5. Who sets tables?
6. Who cleans hotel rooms?
7. Who keeps yards nice?
8. Who works inside?
9. Who works outside?
10. Which jobs do you like?

Receptive Activities
Before doing these activities, make two copies of the picture grid. Cut apart one grid to make picture cards.

1. Give the client the picture grid. Have her match the picture cards to the pictures on the grid. *Where is the _____?*
2. Place the picture cards faceup on the table. Have the client follow your directions. *Touch the _____. Take the _____. Hand me the _____. Point to the _____. Turn over the _____.*
3. Cover three to six pictures on the picture grid. Show the client a picture card and have her tell you where it was on the picture grid. *Where was the _____?*
4. Use classified ads to find job openings in these fields. Glue each picture card to a blank sheet of paper. Cut and paste each job opening on the sheet with its corresponding picture card. *Where should we glue this?*
5. Role-play working one or more of these jobs. For a garden worker, the client could rake or mow a nearby lawn. For a housecleaner, the client could dust the furniture in the room. For a restaurant worker, the client could clean and set a table. For an office helper, the client could help in the school office. For a laundry worker, the client could practice washing PE clothes or cafeteria aprons. For a store employee, the client could practice putting supplies neatly away in cupboards with the labels are facing forward.

Word/Sentence Imitation and Sentence Completion
1. Ask the client to repeat each word after you say it. *Say _____.*
2. Use each word to complete the sentence *They are _____.* Have the client repeat your sentences.
3. Print *The _____ work* on a card. Have the client complete the sentence using the vocabulary words.

Expressive Vocabulary
1. Name each picture.
2. Describe three tasks that housecleaners do.
3. Name three tasks that store employees do.
4. Tell three tasks that office workers do.
5. Describe three tasks that laundry workers do.
6. Name three tasks that restaurant workers do.
7. Tell three tasks that garden workers do.
8. Where could each of these workers work?
9. What kind of job would you like to have?
10. (Cover the pictures.) Name six jobs.

Expressive Activity
Role-play interviewing for one of these jobs. Discuss what to wear to the interview (nice clothes, well-groomed) and what to bring (résumé). Have the client practice greeting you and telling about herself, her job experiences, and why she wants the job. Have the client ask questions about the job, such as about the tasks required, the hours needed, and the pay.

Critical Thinking and Problem Solving
1. Why is it a good idea for a housecleaner to knock before opening a closed door?
2. What should a store employee do if a customer wants to look for something on the shelf she's stocking?
3. What if a customer asks a store employee where something is, but the employee doesn't know?
4. What if the office worker finds a blank page while collating?
5. How does the laundry worker know when the dryer is done?
6. How does the restaurant worker know which tables to clean?
7. What safety rules should a garden worker follow while trimming bushes?
8. What should a worker do if she is sick?
9. What should you consider when choosing the kind of job you want?
10. If you were interviewing for one of these jobs, what skills could you tell the employer that you have?

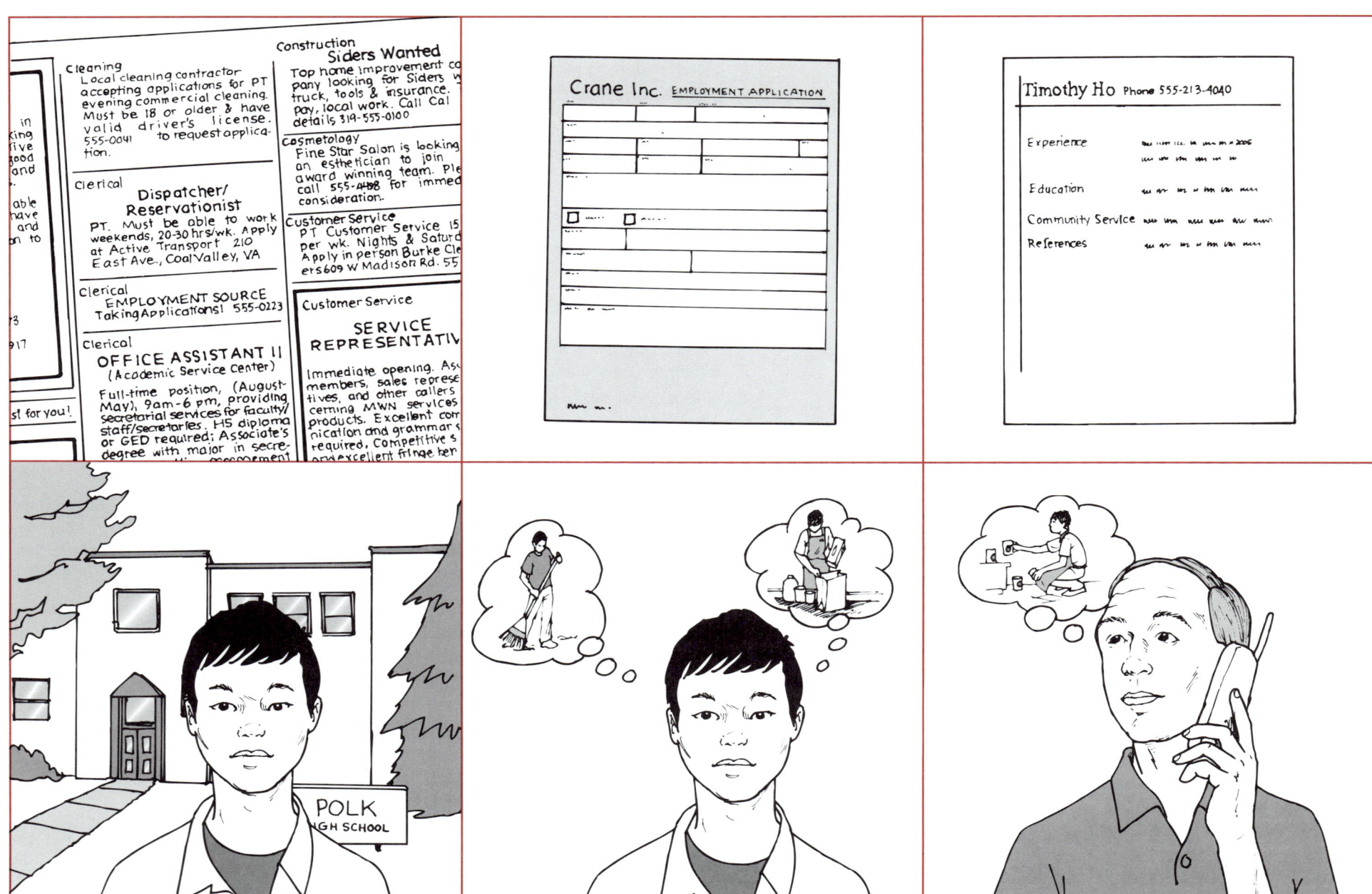

Getting a Job

Receptive Vocabulary
Name each picture the client points to.

1. Point to (the) résumé (application, classified ads, education, experience, references).
2. Which lists job openings?
3. Which lists your previous jobs?
4. What form do you fill out to apply for a job?
5. Who can an employer call to ask about you?
6. Which is the amount of school you've had?
7. Which is the amount of job training you've had?
8. Which two items list your name, address, and phone number?
9. Which should you give to an employer when applying for a job?
10. Which help you get a job?

Receptive Activities
Before doing these activities, make two copies of the picture grid. Cut apart one grid to make picture cards.

1. Give the client the picture grid. Have him match the picture cards to the pictures on the grid. *Where is the _____?*
2. Help the client complete a job application. Match the appropriate picture cards to the parts of the application. *Show me the _____.*
3. Help the client type up a résumé. Match the appropriate picture cards to the parts of the résumé. *Show me the _____.*
4. Place classified ads, a résumé, and an application on the table. Match the picture cards to the items. *Show me the _____.*
5. Place the picture cards faceup on the table. Have the client follow your directions. *Touch (the) _____. Take (the) _____. Hand me (the) _____. Point to (the) _____. Turn over (the) _____.*
6. Cover three to six pictures on the picture grid. Show the client a picture card and have him tell you where it was on the picture grid. *Where was/were (the) _____.*
7. Role-play a job interview. Ask the client to use his résumé to answer the questions. As the "employer," ask the client questions that he can answer by pointing to the correct part of the résumé. *What education have you had? What job experience have you had? Who can I call as a reference?*

Word/Sentence Imitation and Sentence Completion
1. Ask the client to repeat each word after you say it. *Say _____.*
2. Use each word to complete the sentence *I see (a/an/the) _____.* Have the client repeat your sentences.
3. Print *Let's talk about (the) _____* on a card. Have the client complete the sentence using the vocabulary words.

Expressive Vocabulary
1. Name each picture.
2. What do all of these things have in common?
3. What information is given in the classified ads?
4. What information do you put on application?
5. What information do you put on a résumé?
6. Tell about your education.
7. Describe your job experiences.
8. What are references?
9. Who could you put as a reference?
10. (Cover the pictures.) Describe the steps to finding and getting a job.

Expressive Activity
Conduct a mock interview with the client. Discuss what to wear to the interview (nice clothes, well-groomed) and what to bring (résumé). Role-play greetings, asking the client to tell about himself, his education, his job experiences, and why he wants that job. Have the client ask questions about the job, such as about the tasks required, the hours needed, and the pay.

Critical Thinking and Problem Solving
1. When looking at the classified ads, why is it a good idea to consider where a business is located?
2. What else should you consider when looking in the classified ads for a job?
3. Why is it important to make a good impression when completing a job application?
4. Why should you carefully select who you'd like to list as references?
5. Why is it a good idea to be well-groomed and neatly dressed for a job interview?
6. At the beginning of a job interview, why is it a good idea to greet the employer, introduce yourself, and shake hands?
7. When an employer asks you to tell about yourself, what information would be good to share?
8. What experience have you had that would impress an employer?
9. If an employer asks why you want a job, what would be a good answer?
10. What advice would you give to someone who will have a job interview?

Vocabulary at Work: What to Wear to Work
Functional Vocabulary for Adolescents & Adults

What to Wear to Work

Receptive Vocabulary
Name each picture the client points to.

1. Point to the name tag/name badge (vest, watch, apron, collar shirt, hairnet).
2. Which tells the person's name?
3. Which holds back the person's hair?
4. Which tells time?
5. Which protects the person's clothes?
6. Which is a nice shirt?
7. Which are parts of a uniform?
8. Which could people wear while working in a kitchen?
9. Which could people wear while working at a store?
10. Which could people wear while working in an office?

Receptive Activities
Before doing these activities, make two copies of the picture grid. Cut apart one grid to make picture cards.

1. Give the client the picture grid. Have her match the picture cards to the pictures on the grid. *Where is the _____?*
2. Play a game of Bingo. Use pennies as markers.
3. Bring in a real name tag, apron, watch, etc., and have the client match the items to the picture cards. *Where is the _____?*
4. Have the client practice putting on a name tag, apron, watch, etc. *Put on the _____.*
5. Place the items or picture cards faceup on the table. Have the client follow your directions. *Touch the _____. Take the _____. Hand me the _____. Point to the _____. Turn over the _____.*
6. Cover three to six pictures on the picture grid. Show the client a picture card and have her tell you where it was on the picture grid. *Where was the _____?*
7. Look in magazines or on websites for pictures of workers wearing various uniforms. Cut out or print the pictures and glue them to a poster. *Show me the _____.*
8. Visit various worksites. Give the client the picture cards as you talk about what the employees wear to work. *Let's look for a/an _____.*

Word/Sentence Imitation and Sentence Completion
1. Ask the client to repeat each word after you say it. *Say _____.*
2. Use each word to complete the sentence *Put on a/an _____.* Have the client repeat your sentences.
3. Print *I wear a/an _____* on a card. Have the client complete the sentence using the vocabulary words.

Expressive Vocabulary
1. Name each picture.
2. Why do workers wear name tags/name badges?
3. Why do kitchen workers wear aprons?
4. How do you put on a vest?
5. What does a hairnet do?
6. What does a watch do?
7. What could a cook wear at work?
8. What could a store employee wear at work?
9. What could an office worker wear at work?
10. (Cover the pictures.) What could be part of a work uniform?

Expressive Activity
Have the client role-play getting ready for work. Put on needed uniform items such as an apron, a hairnet, a watch, and a name tag. Discuss how to put them on, why to wear each item, and how customers can tell who the workers are.

Critical Thinking and Problem Solving
1. How does a watch help you for work?
2. What could happen if your watch had the wrong time?
3. What could happen if a worker didn't wear her uniform to work?
4. What could happen if a cook didn't wear a hairnet?
5. What could happen if a cook didn't wear an apron?
6. Why do you think some workers have to wear uniforms?
7. Why is it important to wear clean clothes to work?
8. How could you tell if your uniform needed to be cleaned?
9. What could you do if you lost your name badge?
10. When you shop, how do you know who the workers are?

People You Work With

Receptive Vocabulary
Name each picture the client points to.

1. Point to the supervisor (customer, job coach, co-worker).
2. Point to the person who did supported employment (job training).
3. Who is the boss?
4. Who shops?
5. Who assigns tasks?
6. Who teaches tasks?
7. Who works at the same place?
8. Who is learning job skills?
9. Who is paid for working?
10. Who could the worker take a break with?

Receptive Activities
Before doing these activities, make two copies of the picture grid. Cut apart one grid to make picture cards.

1. Give the client the picture grid. Have her match the picture cards to the pictures on the grid. *Where is (the) _____?*
2. Practice doing a job skill at school, such as cleaning tables, delivering teachers' mail, or labeling mailings. *Who is your _____?*
3. Place the picture cards faceup on the table. Have the client follow your directions. *Touch the _____. Take the _____. Hand me the _____. Point to the _____. Turn over the _____.*
4. Cover three to six pictures on the picture grid. Show the client a picture card and have her tell you where it was on the picture grid. *Where was (the) _____?*
5. Visit a store or a fast-food restaurant. Look for the workers, the supervisor, and the customers. *Let's find a _____.*
6. Visit a job training site. Look for the workers, job coach, supervisor, and customers. *Let's find a _____. Who did supported employment? Who did job training?*

Word/Sentence Imitation and Sentence Completion
1. Ask the client to repeat each word after you say it. *Say _____.*
2. Use each word to complete the sentence *She is a _____* or *She did _____*. Have the client repeat your sentences.
3. Print *I work with a _____* and *I did _____* on a card. Have the client complete the sentences using the vocabulary words.

Expressive Vocabulary
1. Name each picture.
2. What do all of these people have in common?
3. What does a supervisor do?
4. What does a job coach do?
5. What does a co-worker do?
6. What does a customer do?
7. How are a supervisor and job coach the same? different?
8. Who can tell you what jobs to do?
9. Who can help you keep your job?
10. (Cover the pictures.) Tell four people you could work with.

Expressive Activity
Have the client practice doing a job skill at school, such as cleaning tables, delivering teachers' mail, or putting address labels on a mailing. Help the client role-play various scenarios, such as greeting a supervisor and asking what job tasks to do, following a job coach's directions, answering a customer's question, asking a job coach for help, and getting along with a co-worker. Talk about the roles of each person and the various relationships.

Critical Thinking and Problem Solving
1. What could you do if you didn't understand your supervisor's directions?
2. What should you do if a customer wants to get something off of a shelf that you're straightening?
3. What if a customer asks you a question and you don't know the answer?
4. What if you finish your job task, but it isn't time to leave work yet?
5. What if you accidentally drop some merchandise and it breaks?
6. What could happen if you don't follow directions?
7. Why is it a good idea to greet your supervisor?
8. Why is it a good idea to get along with your job coach?
9. Why is it a good idea to get along with your co-workers?
10. Tell at least three things good workers do to keep their jobs.

Attributes

Receptive Vocabulary
Name each picture the client points to.

1. Which table is clean? dirty?
2. Which shelf is empty? full?
3. Which dishes are dry? wet?
4. Which table needs to be cleaned?
5. Which shelf needs to be filled?
6. Which dishes need to be dried?
7. How do you like your table to look?
8. Which shelf could you get crackers from?
9. How should dishes look before setting a table?
10. Which of these things should workers notice?

Receptive Activities
Before doing these activities, make two copies of the picture grid. Cut apart one grid to make picture cards.

1. Give the client the picture grid. Have her match the picture cards to the pictures on the grid. *Where is the _____?*
2. Play a game of Bingo. Use pennies as markers.
3. Have the client search around the school for clean and dirty items. *Find a clean/dirty _____ (table, desk, chair, floor, cupboard, bathroom mirror, sink, etc.).*
4. Have the client search around the school for full and empty containers. *Find a full/empty _____ (pencil holder, work folder, paper towel dispenser, trash can, etc.).*
5. Have the client search around the school for wet and dry items. *Find (a) wet/dry _____ (dishes in the sink or on the counter, sponges, towels, tables, countertops, floors, etc.).*
6. Visit a fast-food restaurant or cafeteria. If it's okay with the management, have the client pretend that he works there and check the tables, condiments, and beverage supplies. *Let's look for something that is _____.*

Word/Sentence Imitation and Sentence Completion
1. Ask the client to repeat each word after you say it. *Say _____.*
2. Use each word to complete the sentence *This is _____.* Have the client repeat your sentences.
3. Print *That is _____* on a card. Have the client complete the sentence using the vocabulary words.

Expressive Vocabulary
1. Describe each table (shelf, dish).
2. What should a worker do with a dirty table?
3. What should a worker do with an empty shelf?
4. What should a worker do with wet dishes?
5. Name three things that could get dirty in a hotel room.
6. Name three containers that could be empty in a fast-food restaurant.
7. Name three items that could be wet or dry in a laundry room.
8. What could a worker do if a trash can is full?
9. What could a worker do if the floor is dirty?
10. What chores do you have at home?

Expressive Activity
Have the client practice washing dishes. Talk about which dishes are clean, dirty, wet, or dry. Then have the client check the inventory of the school supplies. Talk about whether the various containers of pencils, paper clips, and paper towels are full or empty.

Critical Thinking and Problem Solving
1. If you worked at a restaurant, what would you do if a customer spilled a soda?
2. Should you clean tables where customers are eating? Why?
3. Should you eat the food off the tables you are cleaning? Why?
4. Why is it important to keep the containers filled at a fast-food restaurant?
5. Why is it important to keep the shelves filled at a store?
6. If you worked at a store, how would you know what goes on an empty shelf?
7. If you worked at a store, what if you didn't know where to find more merchandise that you needed to put on the shelves?
8. If you cleaned laundry at a hotel, why is it a good idea to check the towels before taking them out of the dryer?
9. If you cleaned rooms in a hotel, why is it a good idea to clean everything in the room?
10. How would you know where you had already cleaned?

Vocabulary at Work: Baker Helper

Baker Helper

Receptive Vocabulary
Name each picture the client points to.

1. Point to the apron (pan, batter, hairnet, dough, gloves).
2. Show me which go on hands?
3. Which covers your hair?
4. Which covers your clothes?
5. Which do you bake cookies on?
6. Which do you pour into a pan?
7. After baking, which will become rolls?
8. After baking, which will become cake or muffins?
9. Which would you see at a bakery?
10. Which would a baker wear?

Receptive Activities
Before doing these activities, make two copies of the picture grid. Cut apart one grid to make picture cards.

1. Give the client the picture grid. Have him match the picture cards to the pictures on the grid. *Where is/are the _____?*
2. Play a game of Bingo. Use pennies as markers.
3. Match real items with the picture cards. Put a hairnet, pair of gloves, apron, and baking pan on the table. Point to a picture as you ask *Where is/are the _____?*
4. Ask the clients to try on hairnets, gloves, and an apron. *Put on the _____.*
5. Bake cookies, rolls, or another bakery item. Use the vocabulary words while giving the clients directions during the activity. *Put on the _____. Mix the _____.*
6. Cover three to six pictures on the picture grid. Show the client a picture card and have him tell you where it was on the picture grid. *Where was/were the _____?*
7. Look at classified ads for jobs assisting bakers at local bakeries, grocery stores, restaurants, or cafeterias. *Let's find job openings for a baker helper.*
8. Visit a bakery or the bakery section of a grocery store, restaurant, or cafeteria. Give the picture cards to the client. *Let's find someone who is using (a/an) _____.*

Word/Sentence Imitation and Sentence Completion
1. Ask the client to repeat each word after you say it. *Say _____.*
2. Use each word to complete the sentence *Find the _____.* Have the client repeat your sentences.
3. Print *Use the _____* on a card. Have the client complete the sentence using the vocabulary words.

Expressive Vocabulary
1. Name each picture.
2. What do all of these items have in common?
3. What does a hairnet do?
4. What do gloves do?
5. What does an apron do?
6. Name three foods you could bake on a pan.
7. Name three kinds of dough.
8. Name three kinds of batter.
9. Describe what you would see and smell at a bakery.
10. (Cover the pictures.) Name six items a baker would use.

Expressive Activity
Help the clients bake cookies, rolls, muffins, or another bakery item. Discuss the purpose of wearing gloves, hairnets, and aprons. Ask the clients to describe the items they're using and the steps they're taking to make the food item.

Critical Thinking and Problem Solving
1. What if you have difficulty putting on the food-handling gloves?
2. What if the apron strings get tangled when you try to put on the apron?
3. Why is it a good idea to wash your hands before working with food?
4. What if you smell something burning in the oven?
5. Why is it a good idea to leave spaces between cookies on a pan before baking them?
6. What if you drop a piece of dough on the floor?
7. Why is it a good idea to follow a recipe exactly when making batter?
8. Why can't you eat the cookies that you bake at work?
9. Would you want a job helping a baker? Why?
10. If you were interviewing for a job at a bakery, what skills and experience would you say that you have?

Vocabulary at Work: Dining Room Attendant – Fast-Food Restaurant
Functional Vocabulary for Adolescents & Adults

Dining Room Attendant – Fast-Food Restaurant

Receptive Vocabulary
Name each picture the client points to.

1. Point to the drink dispenser (straws, napkin dispenser, trays, dumpster, condiments).
2. Show where to take out the garbage.
3. Which go in cups?
4. Which machine serves ice and drinks?
5. Which holds napkins?
6. Which includes ketchup and mustard?
7. Which do you carry food on?
8. Which would you see at a fast-food restaurant?
9. Which could need cleaning?
10. Which could need refilling?

Receptive Activities
Before doing these activities, make two copies of the picture grid. Cut apart one grid to make picture cards.

1. Give the client the picture grid. Have him match the picture cards to the pictures on the grid. *Where is/are the _____?*
2. Play a game of Bingo. Use pennies as markers.
3. Place the picture cards faceup on the table. Have the client follow your directions. *Touch the _____. Take the _____. Hand me the _____. Point to the _____. Turn over the _____.*
4. Cover three to six pictures on the picture grid. Show the client a picture card and have him tell you where it was on the picture grid. *Where was/were the _____?*
5. Use classified ads to find job openings at local fast-food restaurants. *Look for dining room attendant job openings.*
6. Visit the school cafeteria or a fast-food restaurant. Give the pictures to the client. *Let's look for (a) _____.*

Word/Sentence Imitation and Sentence Completion
1. Ask the client to repeat each word after you say it. *Say _____.*
2. Use each word to complete the sentence *Check the _____.* Have the client repeat your sentences.
3. Print *Here is/are the _____* on a card. Have the client complete the sentence using the vocabulary words.

Expressive Vocabulary
1. Name each picture.
2. What do all of these items have in common?
3. What is a napkin dispenser for?
4. Name three beverages you could get from a drink dispenser.
5. What is a dumpster for?
6. Name three condiments.
7. What do you do with a straw?
8. What do you do with a tray?
9. Name three fast-food restaurants.
10. (Cover the pictures.) Name six items you'd see at a fast-food restaurant.

Expressive Activity
Have the clients role play working at a fast-food restaurant. Ask the clients use the vocabulary words to describe what they are doing during their day on the job.

Critical Thinking and Problem Solving
1. What would you do if the dumpster was full?
2. When clearing a table, what should you do with food left behind?
3. Why is it a good idea to keep the condiment packets sorted?
4. Why is it a good idea to keep the straws stocked?
5. Why is it a good idea to keep the trays clean?
6. Why should you wait until the customers leave before cleaning their table?
7. How do you know when a napkin dispenser needs more napkins?
8. How do you know when a drink dispenser is out of a soda?
9. Would you want to earn money at a fast-food restaurant? Why?
10. If you were interviewing for a fast-food restaurant job, what skills and experience would you say that you have?

Dining Room Attendant – Restaurant

Receptive Vocabulary
Name each picture the client points to.

1. Point to the place mat (napkin, tablecloth, table tent, silverware, menu).
2. Show what covers a table.
3. What goes under a plate?
4. Which goes on your lap?
5. What utensils do you eat with?
6. Which shows the food choices?
7. What advertises specials?
8. What would you see in a restaurant?
9. What could need cleaning?
10. What could you put on a table?

Receptive Activities
Before doing these activities, make two copies of the picture grid. Cut apart one grid to make picture cards.

1. Place a real tablecloth, table tent, some silverware, etc., on the table. Some restaurants will give you menus you can use, and you can make your own table tent by cutting out pictures of food and gluing them to a sheet of construction paper folded in half. Give the client the picture page and ask her to identify the items in the picture. *Where is the _____?*
2. Bring in a real tablecloth, place mat, napkin, menu, etc. Give the picture page to the client and ask her to make a place setting that looks like the picture. *Pretend you are a dining room attendant. Set the table to look like this.*
3. Bring in a real tablecloth, etc. Without looking at the picture page, have the client follow your directions to set a table. *Put the place mat on the table. Put the plate on the place mat. Put the fork to the left. Put the table tent in the middle of the table.*
4. Bring in a real tablecloth, etc., and role-play working at a restaurant. Ask the client to listen to your cues to set a table. Give less information than you did in the previous activity about what to do with each item. *Get the _____.*
5. Role-play working at a restaurant and clearing a table. Ask the client to clear what you ask. *Pick up the _____.*
6. Visit a restaurant. Use the picture page to find the vocabulary word items. *Let's look for (a) _____.*

Word/Sentence Imitation and Sentence Completion
1. Ask the client to repeat each word after you say it. *Say _____.*
2. Use each word to complete the sentence *I will get (a) _____.* Have the client repeat your sentences.
3. Print *Let's clean the _____* on a card. Have the client complete the sentence using the vocabulary words.

Expressive Vocabulary
1. Name each picture.
2. What do all of these items have in common?
3. How do you put a tablecloth on a table?
4. What goes on a place mat?
5. Name three pieces of silverware.
6. Tell three sections on a menu.
7. Describe what could be advertised on a table tent.
8. What do guests do with a napkin?
9. Name three restaurants.
10. (Cover the pictures.) Name six items you'd see at a restaurant.

Expressive Activity
Role-play working at a restaurant. Some of the clients can pretend to be dining room attendants and others can pretend to be customers. Have the workers describe what they are doing as they clean and set a table, set menus on the place mats, etc. Have the customers ask for items like silverware, napkins, etc.

Critical Thinking and Problem Solving
1. What should you do if the tablecloth you are putting on has a stain on it?
2. When setting a table, what should you do if a fork is bent?
3. When cleaning menus, what should you do if you notice that a page is missing?
4. When cleaning table tents, what should you do if you can't remove some gunk?
5. When clearing tables, why shouldn't you eat leftover food?
6. When setting a table, how can you tell if the tablecloth is even?
7. When setting a table, how do you know how many place mats to set out?
8. When clearing tables, how do you know if a customer is finished?
9. If you were interviewing for a restaurant job, what skills and experience would you say that you have?
10. Would you want to earn money as a dining room attendant? Why?

Vocabulary at Work: Floor Cleaning Supplies
Functional Vocabulary for Adolescents & Adults

Floor Cleaning Supplies

Receptive Vocabulary
Name each picture the client points to.

1. Point to the dust mop (vacuum, broom, dustpan, mop bucket, mop).
2. Which sweeps?
3. Which mops?
4. Which vacuums?
5. Which goes with the broom?
6. Which goes with the mop?
7. Which dry mops the floor?
8. Which can get wet?
9. Which stay dry?
10. Which help clean floors?

Receptive Activities
Before doing these activities, make two copies of the picture grid. Cut apart one grid to make picture cards.

1. Give the client the picture grid. Have her match the picture cards to the pictures on the grid. *Where is the _____?*
2. Play a game of Bingo. Use pennies as markers.
3. Get a real broom, mop, etc. Give a picture card to the client and have her put it by the matching item. *Find the _____.*
4. Spill something on the floor, such as pencil sharpener shavings or hole-punch dots. Use the vocabulary words to ask the client to clean up the mess. *Get the broom. Use the dust mop. Turn on the vacuum.*
5. Ask the client to clean the floor in your room, in the cafeteria, or in another room. Use the vocabulary words while giving directions during the activity. *Get the dustpan. Use the broom.*
6. Use ads from a grocery store, a discount department store, a drug store, or on a website that contains floor cleaning supplies. *Find a _____.*
7. Use classified ads to find jobs cleaning floors at places such as hospitals, hotels, hair salons, restaurants, or other businesses. *Let's find jobs for floor cleaners.*
8. Visit a drug store or a grocery store. Use the pictures as a shopping list. *Let's look for a _____.*

Word/Sentence Imitation and Sentence Completion
1. Ask the client to repeat each word after you say it. *Say _____.*
2. Use each word to complete the sentence *I use a_____.* Have the client repeat your sentences.
3. Print *I clean with a _____* on a card. Have the client complete the sentence using the vocabulary words.

Expressive Vocabulary
1. Name each picture.
2. What do all of these items have in common?
3. Describe how to use a broom and a dustpan.
4. Tell how to use a mop and a mop bucket.
5. Explain how to use a dust mop.
6. Describe how to use a vacuum.
7. What's the difference between a mop and a dust mop?
8. What's the difference between cleaning tile and cleaning carpet?
9. Name five work sites that have their floors cleaned.
10. (Cover the pictures.) Name six items you could use to clean floors.

Expressive Activity
Have two clients role-play interviewing for a job cleaning floors. Have one client pretend to be the employer, and the other client can pretend to be the job applicant. Have them practice greeting one another, and ask the job applicant to use the vocabulary words to tell about herself, her job experiences, and why she wants the job.

Critical Thinking and Problem Solving
1. How would you clean a tile floor? carpet?
2. Why is it a good idea to sweep or dust mop a floor before mopping it?
3. How do you know where you have already swept?
4. What do you do if a mop doesn't clean a spot on the floor?
5. How do you know when the mop needs to be rinsed out?
6. How do you know when you need to change the water in your mop bucket?
7. What do you need to be careful about when the floor is wet?
8. What do you do if the vacuum makes a funny sound?
9. Would you want a job cleaning floors? Why?
10. If you were interviewing for a job that includes cleaning floors, what skills and experience would you say that you have?

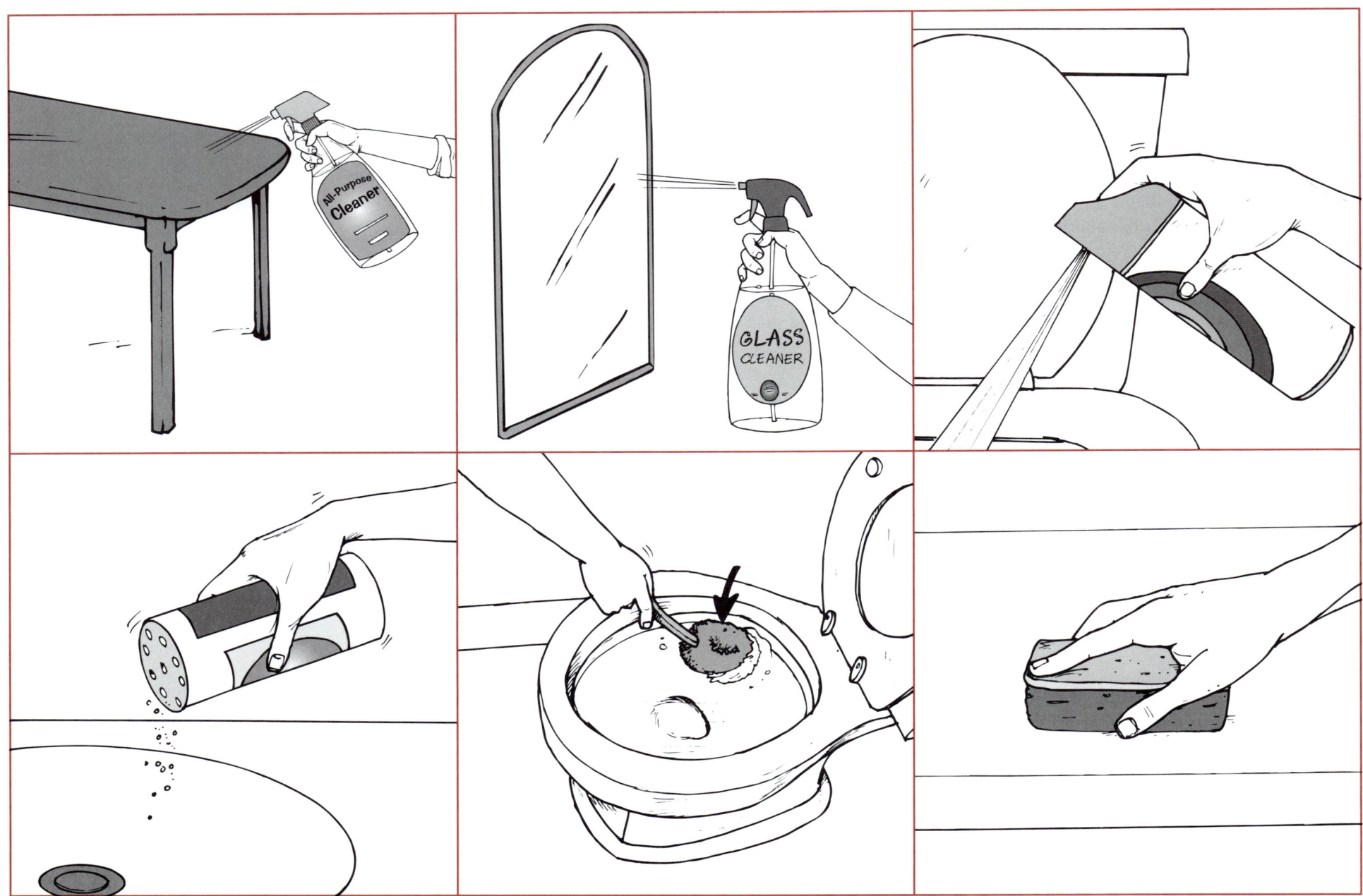

Vocabulary at Work: Housecleaning Supplies
Functional Vocabulary for Adolescents & Adults

Housecleaning Supplies

Receptive Vocabulary
Name each picture the client points to.

1. Point to the glass cleaner (sponge, all-purpose cleaner, toilet bowl cleaner, toilet bowl brush, cleanser).
2. Which clean a counter?
3. Which clean a bathtub?
4. Which cleans a mirror?
5. Which two items clean a toilet?
6. Which cleans a window?
7. Which clean a sink?
8. Which clean a kitchen?
9. Which clean a bathroom?
10. Which do you know how to use?

Receptive Activities
Before doing these activities, make two copies of the picture grid. Cut apart one grid to make picture cards.

1. Give the client the picture grid. Have him match the picture cards to the pictures on the grid. *Where is the _____?*
2. Play a game of Bingo. Use pennies as markers.
3. Place a real bottle of all-purpose cleaner, bottle of window cleaner, toilet bowl brush, etc., on the table. Give a picture card to the client and have him put it by the matching item. *Find the _____.*
4. Help the client clean a bathroom or a kitchen. Use the vocabulary words while giving directions during the activity. *Get the _____. Spray the _____.*
5. Use ads from a grocery store or a discount store, or look on a website that contains ads for cleaning supplies. *Find (a/an) _____.*
6. Use classified ads to find job openings cleaning places such as hospitals and hotels. *Let's look for housecleaning jobs.*
7. Visit a drug store or a grocery store. Use the pictures as a shopping list. *Let's look for (a/an) _____.*

Word/Sentence Imitation and Sentence Completion
1. Ask the client to repeat each word after you say it. *Say _____.*
2. Use each word to complete the sentence *I use (a) _____.* Have the client repeat your sentences.
3. Print *I clean with (a) _____* on a card. Have the client complete the sentence using the vocabulary words.

Expressive Vocabulary
1. Name each picture.
2. What do all of these items have in common?
3. Name three items you can clean with all-purpose cleaner.
4. Describe how to clean a mirror.
5. Tell how to clean a toilet.
6. Explain how to use cleanser to clean a sink.
7. Describe how to rinse out a sponge.
8. Name three places that have rest rooms.
9. Describe the steps to cleaning a whole bathroom.
10. (Cover the pictures.) Name six items you would need to clean a rest room.

Expressive Activity
Work with the clients to clean a bathroom together. Ask the clients to talk about the supplies they're using and to describe how to clean each particular item and area in the bathroom.

Critical Thinking and Problem Solving
1. Why is it a good idea to knock on a closed door before going in a room to clean it?
2. What could you do if you run out of window cleaner?
3. What if the toilet overflows?
4. What if the sink is clogged?
5. How can you tell you're running out of cleanser?
6. How can you tell if your sponge is too wet? What could you do?
7. How can you tell if your sponge is getting dirty? What could you do?
8. Why is it a good idea to wear gloves while cleaning a bathroom?
9. Would you want a housecleaning job? Why?
10. If you were interviewing for a housecleaning job, what skills and experience would you say that you have?

Laundry Worker

Receptive Vocabulary
Name each picture the client points to.

1. Point to the laundry detergent (washing machine, dryer).
2. Show me who is folding (ironing, sorting).
3. Which washes laundry?
4. Which dries laundry?
5. Which soap goes in the washing machine?
6. Which smoothes wrinkles out of laundry?
7. What is dividing linens into piles?
8. What could you do with clean laundry?
9. Which are done at a hotel?
10. Which are done with your clothes?

Receptive Activities
Before doing these activities, make two copies of the picture grid. Cut apart one grid to make picture cards.

1. Give the client the picture grid. Have her match the picture cards to the pictures on the grid. *Where is (the) _____?*
2. Play a game of Bingo. Use pennies as markers.
3. Find housekeeping tasks that need to be done—perhaps washing PE clothes, the cafeteria workers' aprons, or a volunteer's clothes. Use the vocabulary during the activity. *Show me the _____. Sort the _____. Fold the _____. Iron the _____.*
4. Use classified ads to find jobs doing laundry at nearby hotels, hospitals, convalescent hospitals, or at full-service Laundromats. *Let's find laundry worker job openings.*
5. Cover three to six pictures on the picture grid. Show the client a picture card and have her tell you where it was on the picture grid. *Where was (the) _____.*
6. Visit the laundry room at a hotel, a hospital, a Laundromat, or someone's home. Give the picture cards to the client. *Let's look for (a) _____* or *Let's look for someone who is _____.*

Word/Sentence Imitation and Sentence Completion
1. Ask the client to repeat each word after you say it. *Say _____.*
2. Use each word to complete the sentence *I see (a) _____.* Have the client repeat your sentences.
3. Print *Here is (a) _____* on a card. Have the client complete the sentence using the vocabulary words.

Expressive Vocabulary
1. Name each picture.
2. What do all of these items have in common?
3. Describe how to use a washing machine.
4. Tell how to use a dryer.
5. Explain how to use laundry detergent.
6. Describe how to sort laundry.
7. Tell how to fold towels.
8. Explain how to iron a shirt.
9. What are the steps to washing your clothes?
10. (Cover the pictures.) Name six items used to clean, dry, and iron clothing.

Expressive Activity
Have two clients role-play interviewing for a job as laundry worker. Have one client pretend to be the employer, and the other client pretend to be the job applicant. Have them practice greeting one another, and ask the job applicant to use the vocabulary words to tell about herself, her job experiences, and why she wants the job.

Critical Thinking and Problem Solving
1. Why should laundry be sorted before washing it?
2. What could you do before washing if a shirt has a stain on it?
3. How do you know whether to wash the laundry in hot, warm, or cold water?
4. What could happen if you put too much laundry detergent in the washing machine?
5. What should you do if the washing machine makes a funny noise?
6. How do you know if the laundry in the dryer is done?
7. What are some safety rules to follow when using an iron?
8. What could happen if you hold an iron on a piece of laundry too long?
9. Would you want a job as a laundry worker? Why?
10. If you were interviewing for a job cleaning laundry, what skills and experience would you say that you have?

Lawn and Garden Tools

Receptive Vocabulary
Name each picture the client points to.

1. Point to the edger (rake, weed whacker, lawn mower, clippers, trowel).
2. Show me which cuts grass?
3. Which cuts bushes?
4. Which cut the edge of the grass?
5. Which rakes up leaves?
6. Which digs holes?
7. Which are sharp?
8. Which do you have at your home?
9. Which would a gardener or lawn care worker use?
10. Which are lawn and garden tools?

Receptive Activities
Before doing these activities, make two copies of the picture grid. Cut apart one grid to make picture cards.

1. Give the client the picture grid. Have him match the picture cards to the pictures on the grid. *Where is the _____?*
2. Help the client work in a yard raking, mowing, and trimming, or create a small garden by planting vegetables or small flowers. Use the vocabulary while giving directions during the activity. *Get the _____. Use the _____.*
3. Cover three to six pictures on the picture grid. Show the client a picture card and have him tell you where it was on the picture grid. *Where was the _____?*
4. Use classified ads to find job openings for garden workers at places such as parks, athletic fields, college campuses, cemeteries, nurseries, hotels, and golf courses. *Let's find job openings for garden workers. Find groundskeeper. Look for maintenance worker.*
5. Use ads from hardware stores or lawn and garden stores, or look on a website that contains lawn and garden tools. *Find (a/an) _____.*
6. Visit a store that sells lawn and garden tools. Use the pictures as a shopping list. *Let's look for (a/an) _____.*

Word/Sentence Imitation and Sentence Completion
1. Ask the client to repeat each word after you say it. *Say _____.*
2. Use each word to complete the sentence *I use the _____.* Have the client repeat your sentences.
3. Print *Get the _____* on a card. Have the client complete the sentence using the vocabulary words.

Expressive Vocabulary
1. Name each picture.
2. What do all of these items have in common?
3. Tell the steps to raking leaves.
4. Describe how to mow a lawn.
5. Explain how to trim the edge of a lawn.
6. Tell how to trim bushes.
7. Describe how to plant a small plant.
8. What is the difference between a weed whacker and an edger?
9. Name three grassy places that need upkeep.
10. (Cover the pictures.) What tools does a garden worker or groundskeeper use?

Expressive Activity
Have two clients role-play interviewing for a job as a garden worker or groundskeeper. Have one client pretend to be the employer, and the other client can pretend to be the job applicant. Have them practice greeting one another, and ask the job applicant to use the vocabulary words to tell about himself, his job experiences, and why he wants the job.

Critical Thinking and Problem Solving
1. What are some safety rules to follow when using clippers?
2. How can you tell if a plant is a weed?
3. What should you do with weeds in a flower or vegetable garden?
4. When raking leaves, how do you know when you're finished?
5. When mowing a lawn, how do you know where you've already mowed?
6. When digging a hole, how do you decide whether to use a trowel or a shovel?
7. When planting new plants, how do you know how far apart to plant them?
8. How do you know if a fruit or vegetable is ripe enough to pick?
9. Would you be interested in a job as a garden worker or groundskeeper? Why?
10. If you were interviewing for a garden worker or groundskeeper job, what skills and experience would you say that you have?

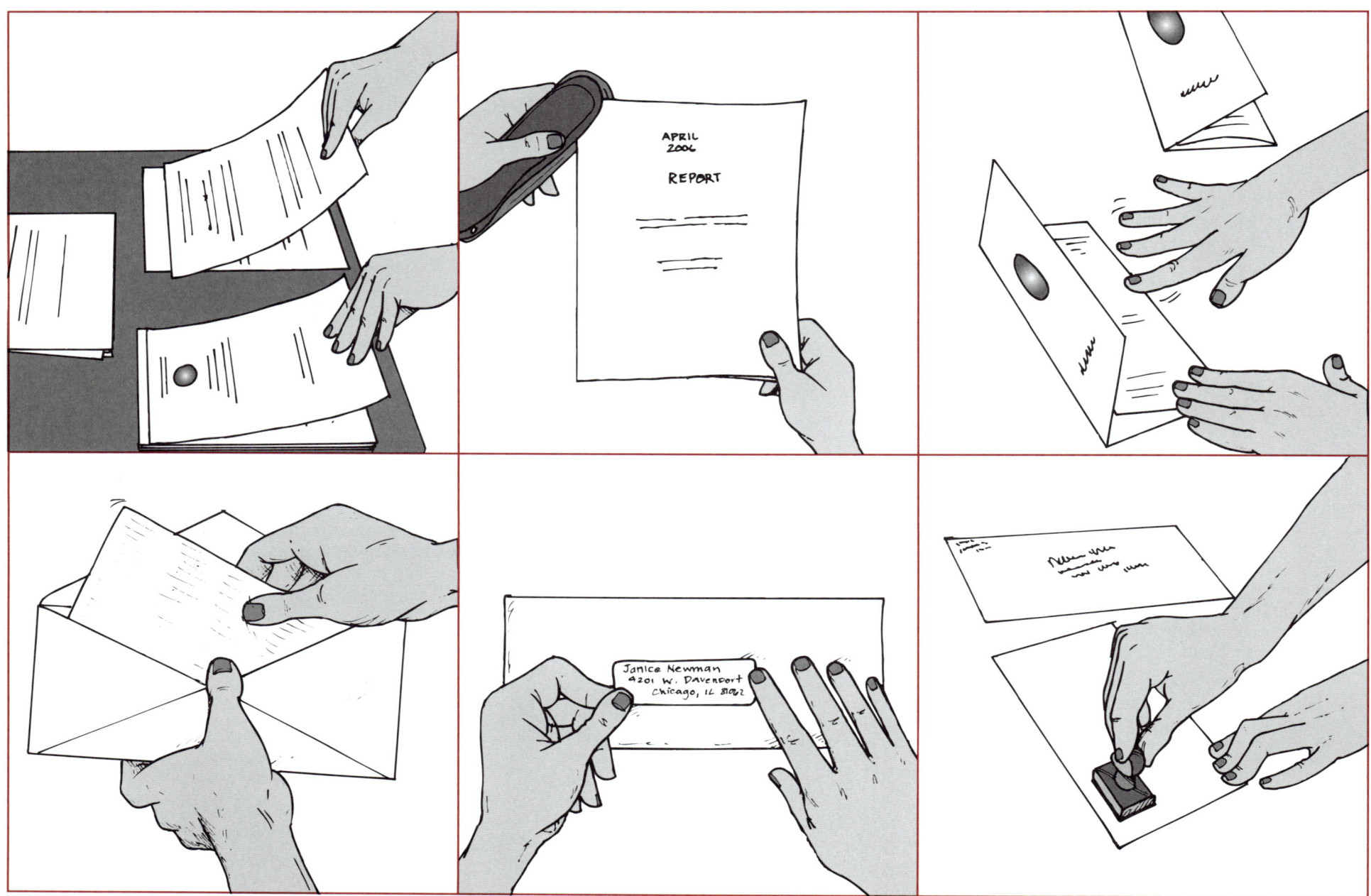

Vocabulary at Work: Office Helper Tasks
Functional Vocabulary for Adolescents & Adults

Office Helper Tasks

Receptive Vocabulary
Name each picture the client points to.

1. Point to folding (collating, stamping, stuffing, labeling, stapling).
2. Show me which you do with a stapler.
3. Which do you do with envelopes?
4. Which do you do with a rubber stamp?
5. Which do you do with address labels?
6. Which do you do to put pages in order?
7. Which shows what to do with a flat brochure?
8. Which tasks are done in an office?
9. Which have you done?
10. Which would you like to do?

Receptive Activities
Before doing these activities, make two copies of the picture grid. Cut apart one grid to make picture cards.

1. Give the client the picture grid. Have her match the picture cards to the pictures on the grid. *Where is the _____?*
2. Play a pantomime game using the picture cards or real items. *Show me how you _____.*
3. Find clerical tasks for your clients to do, such as collating school worksheets, labeling flyers for the school or a nearby realtor or dentist, or processing mail for a local charity. Use the vocabulary words while giving the clients directions during the activity.
4. Cover three to six pictures on the picture grid. Show the client a picture card and have her tell you where it was on the picture grid. *Where was _____?*
5. Use classified ads to find job openings helping in an office at local businesses or schools. *Look for office helper job openings.*
6. Visit an office. Give the picture cards to the client. *Let's find someone who is _____.*

Word/Sentence Imitation and Sentence Completion
1. Ask the client to repeat each word after you say it. *Say _____.*
2. Use each word to complete the sentence *He is _____*. Have the client repeat your sentences.
3. Print *I _____ the papers* on a card. Have the client complete the sentence using the vocabulary words.

Expressive Vocabulary
1. Tell what is happening in each picture.
2. What do all of these tasks have in common?
3. Describe how to collate papers.
4. Tell how to staple papers.
5. Explain how to fold papers.
6. Describe how to stuff and seal an envelope.
7. Tell how and where to put an address label on an envelope.
8. Explain how and where to stamp the return address on an envelope.
9. Name three offices where people do this kind of work.
10. (Cover the pictures.) Name six tasks that an office worker does.

Expressive Activity
Find clerical tasks for your clients to do, such as collating school worksheets, labeling flyers for the school or a nearby realtor or dentist, or processing mail for a local charity. Ask the clients to describe what they are doing and what their co-workers are doing. For more language, purposefully give them small amounts to do at a time so they need to request more. For example, if labeling envelopes, only give a few envelopes and labels. When they finish, they must ask for more.

Critical Thinking and Problem Solving
1. What do office workers wear to work?
2. What if you were collating and there were some pages missing?
3. What if your stapler runs out of staples?
4. What if you folded a brochure crookedly?
5. What if a letter doesn't fit into an envelope?
6. What if a label creases when you put it on an envelope?
7. What clerical tasks can you do?
8. Why is it important to dress nicely at an office?
9. Would you want a job as an office worker? Why?
10. If you were interviewing for an office worker job, what skills and experience would you say that you have?

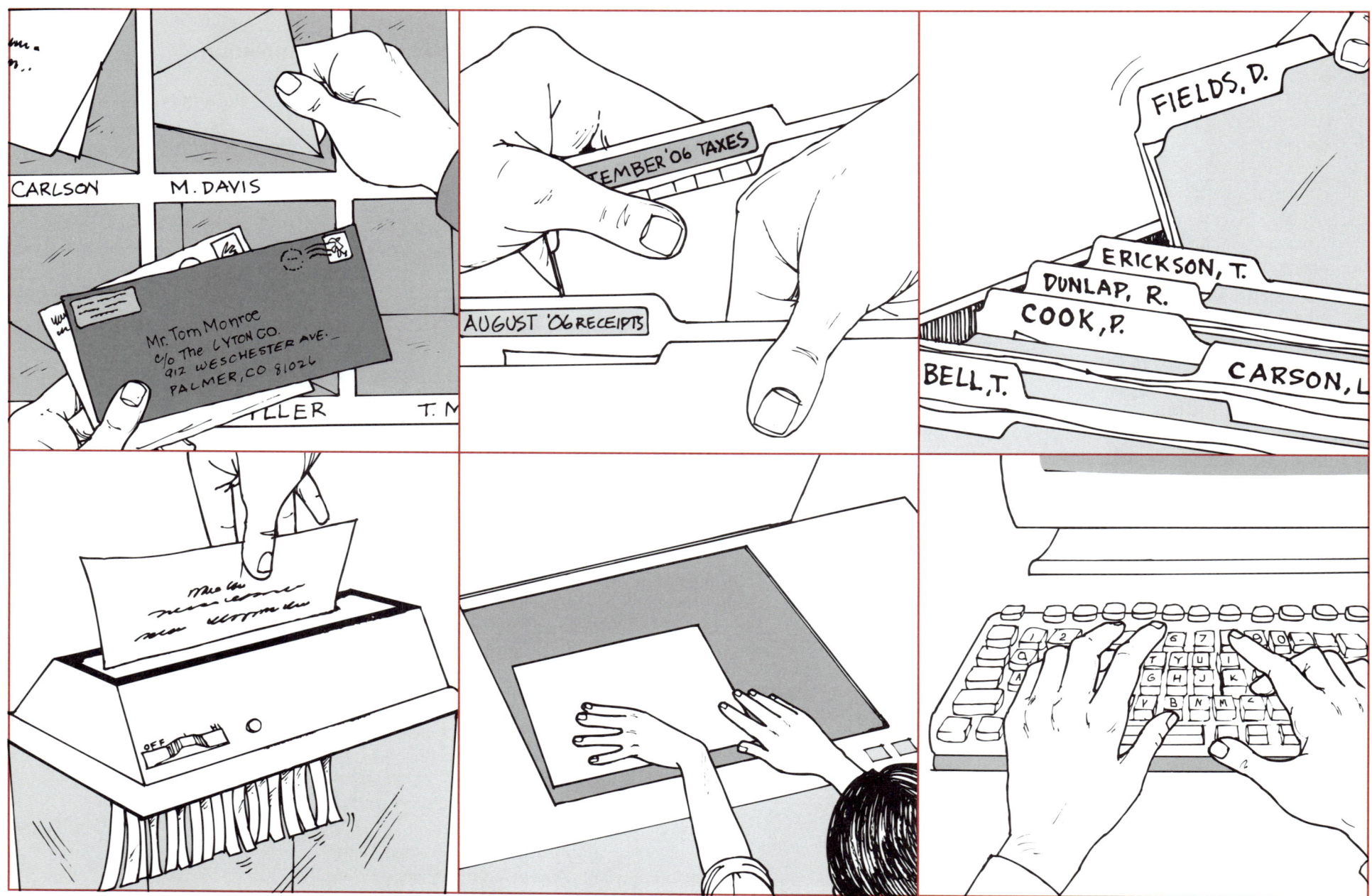

Vocabulary at Work: Office Helper Advanced Tasks
Functional Vocabulary for Adolescents & Adults

Office Helper Advanced Tasks

Receptive Vocabulary
Name each picture the client points to.

1. Point to sorting (alphabetizing, typing, filing, copying, and shredding).
2. Show me what you do to make more of the same page.
3. How do you get rid of old papers?
4. How do you put information on a computer?
5. How do you divide the incoming mail?
6. Which do you do with file folders?
7. Which shows how to organize files?
8. Which tasks are done in an office?
9. Which have you done before?
10. Which would you like to do?

Receptive Activities
Before doing these activities, make two copies of the picture grid. Cut apart one grid to make picture cards.

1. Give the client the picture grid. Have her match the picture cards to the pictures on the grid. *Where is _____?*
2. Play a game of Bingo. Use pennies as markers.
3. Find clerical tasks for your clients to do, like alphabetizing emergency cards or student papers, filing student papers into folders, photocopying worksheets, or typing names and addresses into a database. Use the vocabulary words while giving the clients directions during the activity. *Sort the mail. Alphabetize these cards. File these folders. Copy these worksheets. Type these addresses.*
4. Cover three to six pictures on the picture grid. Show the client a picture card and have her tell you where it was on the picture grid. *Where was _____?*
5. Use classified ads to find job openings helping in an office at local businesses or schools. *Look for office helper job openings.*
6. Visit an office. Give the picture cards to the client. *Let's find someone who is _____.*

Word/Sentence Imitation and Sentence Completion
1. Ask the client to repeat each word after you say it. *Say _____.*
2. Use each word to complete the sentence *She is _____.* Have the client repeat your sentences.
3. Print *I will _____ the papers* on a card. Have the client complete the sentence using the vocabulary words.

Expressive Vocabulary
1. Tell what is happening in each picture.
2. What do all of these tasks have in common?
3. Explain how to sort mail.
4. Describe how to file papers.
5. Tell how to alphabetize papers.
6. Explain how to shred papers.
7. Describe how to copy pages.
8. Name three kinds of information that could be typed on a computer.
9. Name three offices where people do this clerical work.
10. (Cover the pictures.) Name six tasks that an office worker does.

Expressive Activity
Find clerical tasks for your clients to do, such as alphabetizing emergency cards or student papers, filing student papers into folders, photocopying worksheets, or typing names and addresses into a database. Ask the clients to describe the activity. For added language opportunities, plant problems into the task. For example, have an alphabet letter missing in the filing cabinet or box, a student folder missing when filing papers, or the photocopy machine run out of paper. Have the client ask for help with each obstacle.

Critical Thinking and Problem Solving
1. When sorting mail, what if one name isn't on your list?
2. When filing, what if a folder is missing?
3. When alphabetizing by names, do you use the person's first or last name?
4. When alphabetizing, what do you do if two names start with the same letter?
5. When shredding, what do you do if the machine starts to overheat?
6. When copying, what if the machine runs out of paper?
7. When copying, what if the machine shows an error message?
8. When typing, what if you can't read the writing you are to type?
9. Would you want a job as an office helper? Why?
10. If you were interviewing for an office worker job, what skills and experience would you say that you have?

Stock Clerk

Receptive Vocabulary
Name each picture the client points to.

1. Point to the warehouse (go backs, merchandise, end cap, aisle, bar code).
2. Which is sold at stores?
3. Which is like a hallway?
4. Which is at the end of the aisle?
5. Which products need to go back on shelves?
6. Where does the store keep extra merchandise?
7. Which label tells the price and product information?
8. Which have you seen at a grocery store?
9. Which have you seen at a department store?
10. Which have you seen at a drug store?

Receptive Activities
Before doing these activities, make two copies of the picture grid. Cut apart one grid to make picture cards.

1. Give the client the picture grid. Have her match the picture cards to the pictures on the grid. *Where is the _____?*
2. Play a game of Bingo. Use pennies as markers.
3. Pretend your room is a store. Have the client find "merchandise" on the shelves, and then have her practice putting "go backs" back on the shelves. *Where is the merchandise? Get the go backs.*
4. Place the picture cards faceup on the table. Have the client follow your directions. *Touch the _____. Take the _____. Hand me the _____. Point to the _____. Turn over the _____.*
5. Use classified ads to find job openings at nearby stores. *Let's find stock clerk job openings.*
6. Visit a grocery store, a discount store, a department store, or a drug store. Give the picture cards to the client. *Let's look for (a/an) _____.*

Word/Sentence Imitation and Sentence Completion
1. Ask the client to repeat each word after you say it. *Say _____.*
2. Use each word to complete the sentence *I see (a/an) _____.* Have the client repeat your sentences.
3. Print *A store has (a/an) _____* on a card. Have the client complete the sentence using the vocabulary words.

Expressive Vocabulary
1. Name each picture.
2. What do all of these items have in common?
3. Name three merchandise items you'd find at a discount store.
4. Describe a warehouse.
5. Tell three aisles you'd find at a grocery store.
6. Explain what an end cap is.
7. Describe how a bar code is used.
8. Tell what a worker does with go backs.
9. Name three stores that have stock clerks.
10. (Cover the pictures.) Name three places a worker could find merchandise.

Expressive Activity
Pretend your room is a store. Designate one area to be the "warehouse." Have her take "merchandise" out of the warehouse and put it on shelves, find "merchandise" on the shelves, and practice putting "go backs" back on the shelves. Have her use the vocabulary words to explain what she's doing throughout the activity.

Critical Thinking and Problem Solving
1. What if you were working in the warehouse and couldn't reach the top shelf?
2. What if a customer wanted to get by you when you were working in an aisle?
3. Why is it a good idea to keep the end caps filled and neat?
4. Why is it a good idea to learn the names of the products as you put away go backs?
5. Why is it a good idea to learn which aisle the products are in?
6. What if a customer asked you which aisle a product was in, but you didn't know?
7. Why must the bar code on a product match the bar code on the shelf?
8. How does the bar code help keep track of inventory?
9. Would you want a job at a retail store stocking shelves? Why?
10. If you were interviewing for a job stocking shelves, what skills and experience would you say that you have?

Vocabulary at Work: Stock Clerk – Clothing Store
Functional Vocabulary for Adolescents & Adults

Stock Clerk – Clothing Store

Receptive Vocabulary
Name each picture the client points to.

1. Point to the sensor (dressing room, rack).
2. Who is hanging (folding, sizing)?
3. Where can you try on clothes?
4. Where do you hang clothes?
5. Which is a small alarm?
6. What do you do with clothes before putting them on a shelf?
7. Which is a hanger used for?
8. How do you organize the different sizes?
9. Which would you see at a clothing store?
10. Which would you like to do for work?

Receptive Activities
Before doing these activities, make two copies of the picture grid. Cut apart one grid to make picture cards.

1. Give the client the picture grid. Have him match the picture cards to the pictures on the grid. *Where is (the) _____?*
2. Play a game of Bingo. Use pennies as markers.
3. Write sizes on two sets of cards, one with numerical sizes and the other with S, M, L, and XL. Ask the client to size each stack, putting the sizes in order from smallest to largest. *Size these items.*
4. Bring in real clothing items (different sizes) and hangers, both regular and ones with clips. Ask the clients to fold, hang, and size the items. *Fold the _____. Hang the _____. Size these _____.*
5. Use classified ads to find job openings at nearby clothing stores. *Let's find job openings for stock clerks at a clothing store.*
6. Cover three to six pictures on the picture grid. Show the client a picture card and have him tell you where it was on the picture grid. *Where was (the) _____.*
7. Visit a clothing store. Give the picture cards to the client. *Find (a) _____* or *Let's look for someone who is _____.*

Word/Sentence Imitation and Sentence Completion
1. Ask the client to repeat each word after you say it. *Say _____.*
2. Use each word to complete the sentence *I see (a) _____.* Have the client repeat your sentences.
3. Print *Here is (a) _____* on a card. Have the client complete the sentence using the vocabulary words.

Expressive Vocabulary
1. Name each picture.
2. What do all of these items and tasks have in common?
3. Describe how to fold a shirt.
4. Name three clothing items you can hang.
5. Tell how to put the clothes in order by size.
6. Describe what people do in a dressing room.
7. Explain how a sensor works.
8. Tell what workers could do with a rack.
9. Name three clothing stores where people do this kind of work.
10. (Cover the pictures.) Name three tasks workers do at a clothing store.

Expressive Activity
Bring in different sizes of clothing and different styles of hangers. Have the clients pretend they work at a clothing store. Instruct them to fold and hang clothing, put sizes in order from smallest to largest, and sort different types of hangers. Ask the clients to describe what they're doing throughout the activity.

Critical Thinking and Problem Solving
1. What should you be careful about when pushing a rack?
2. Why is it a good idea to knock on a dressing room door before opening it?
3. Why is it a good idea to smooth out a shirt before folding it?
4. Why is it a good idea to check the sleeves when hanging shirts?
5. Why is it a good idea to hang all the clothes facing the same direction?
6. Why is it a good idea to be nicely dressed and groomed when working at a clothing store?
7. How does a sensor prevent people from stealing clothes?
8. How does putting the clothes in order by size make shopping easier?
9. Would you like to work at a clothing store? Why?
10. If you were interviewing for a job at a clothing store, what skills and experience would you say that you have?

Vocabulary at Work: Stock Clerk Tasks
Functional Vocabulary for Adolescents & Adults

Stock Clerk Tasks

Receptive Vocabulary
Name each picture the client points to.

1. Point to who is bagging (stocking, lifting, matching, pricing, facing/fronting).
2. Which shows putting merchandise in bags?
3. Which shows putting prices on products?
4. Which shows putting merchandise on shelves?
5. Which shows looking at the label and bar code?
6. Which shows moving merchandise to the front of a shelf?
7. Which shows getting boxes from the ground?
8. Which of these are done at a store?
9. Which of these could you do?
10. Which would you like to do?

Receptive Activities
Before doing these activities, make two copies of the picture grid. Cut apart one grid to make picture cards.

1. Give the client the picture grid. Have her match the picture cards to the pictures on the grid. *Where is _____?*
2. Play a game of Bingo. Use pennies as markers.
3. Ask the client to perform retail store-like tasks that you need done, like putting away school supplies that you ordered; putting supplies in bags; or straightening shelves in your class, an office, or in the school library. Use the vocabulary words while giving the client instructions throughout the activity. *Stock these shelves. Face the items on the shelf. Match the items to the shelves. Bag these items.*
4. Place the picture cards faceup on the table. Have the client follow your directions. *Touch the _____. Take the _____. Hand me the _____. Point to the _____. Turn over the _____.*
5. Use classified ads to find job openings at local stores. *Find job openings for stock clerks.*
6. Visit a store. Give the picture cards to the client. *Let's look for someone who is _____.*

Word/Sentence Imitation and Sentence Completion
1. Ask the client to repeat each word after you say it. *Say _____.*
2. Use each word to complete the sentence *He is _____ merchandise.* Have the client repeat your sentences.
3. Print *I am _____ merchandise* on a card. Have the client complete the sentence using the vocabulary words.

Expressive Vocabulary
1. What is each person doing?
2. What do all of these tasks have in common?
3. Describe how to stock shelves.
4. Tell what you need to look for to match products.
5. Explain two things you need to do when facing shelves.
6. Describe how to price items.
7. Tell what to do with a new box of merchandise.
8. Explain how to bag groceries.
9. Name three stores where people do this kind of work.
10. (Cover the pictures.) What tasks would a stock clerk at a retail store have to do?

Expressive Activity
Ask the clients to perform retail store-like tasks that you need done, such as putting away school supplies that you ordered, straightening shelves in your class or office or in the school library, and putting supplies in bags. Encourage the clients to use the vocabulary words to describe the tasks they're doing.

Critical Thinking and Problem Solving
1. What are some safety rules to follow when lifting big boxes?
2. What if one of the bottles you were stocking on a shelf was leaking?
3. When stocking shelves, what if you couldn't find where to put an item?
4. When matching products, does the size of the container matter? Why?
5. When facing products, which way should the label face? Why?
6. When pricing merchandise, why should you double-check the price before putting it on a product?
7. When bagging groceries, why do you need to be careful that the bag doesn't get too heavy?
8. When bagging merchandise, why should fragile items be packed carefully?
9. Would you want to work in a retail store? Why?
10. If you were interviewing for a job in a retail store, what skills and experience would you say that you have?

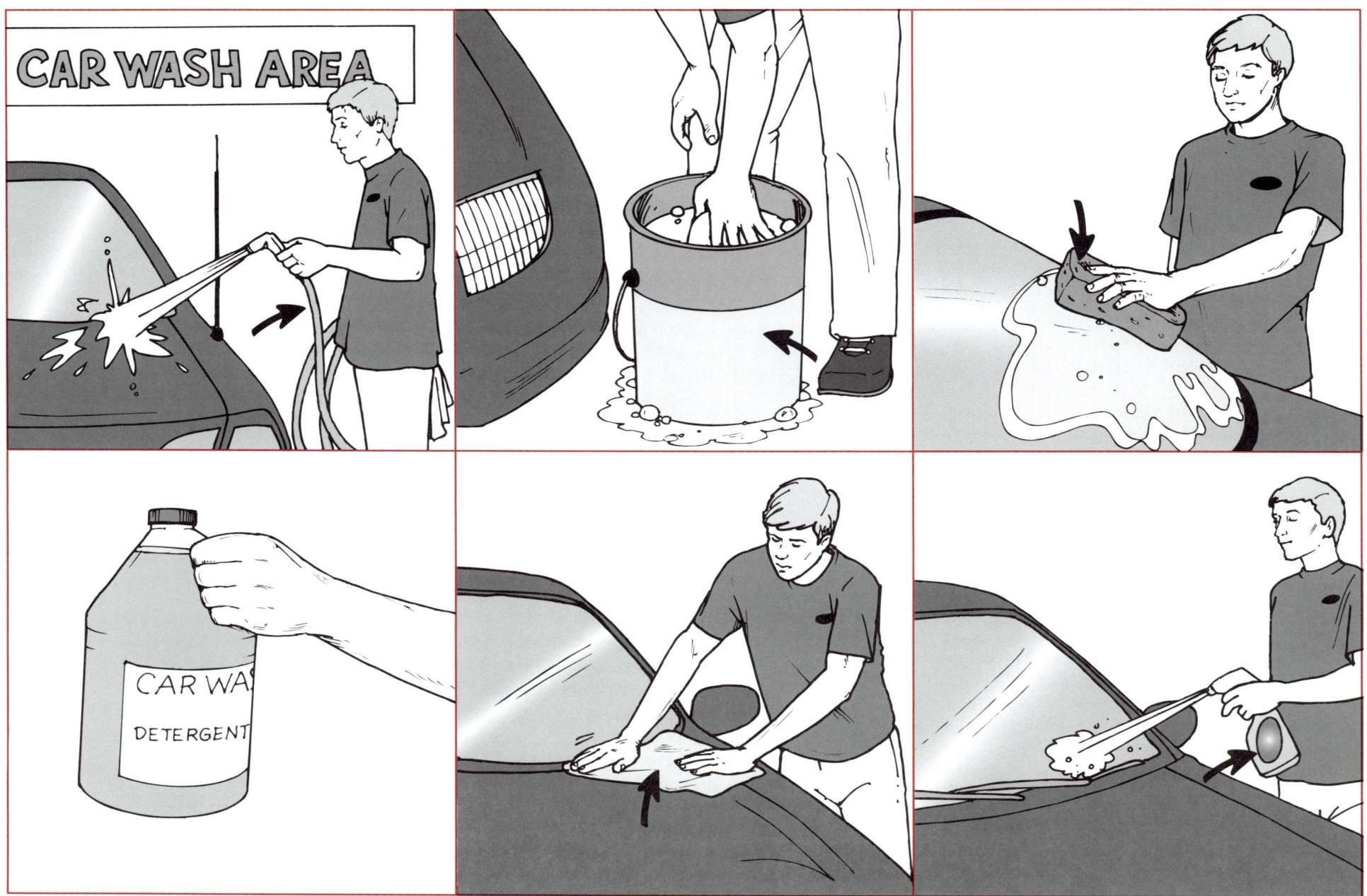

Vehicle Cleaning Supplies

Receptive Vocabulary
Name each picture the client points to.

1. Point to the hose (chamois towel, window cleaner, sponge, bucket, car wash detergent).
2. Which soap do you use to clean a car?
3. Which hold soapy water?
4. Which rinses the car?
5. Which do you use to wipe the car?
6. Which dries the car?
7. Which clean the windows?
8. Which clean the mirrors?
9. Which would you see at a car wash?
10. Which do you need to clean a car?

Receptive Activities
Before doing these activities, make two copies of the picture grid. Cut apart one grid to make picture cards.

1. Give the client the picture grid. Have him match the picture cards to the pictures on the grid. *Where is the _____?*
2. Place the picture cards faceup on the table. Have the client follow your directions. *Touch the _____. Take the _____. Hand me the _____. Point to the _____. Turn over the _____.*
3. Cover three to six pictures on the picture grid. Show the client a picture card and have him tell you where it was on the picture grid. *Where was the _____?*
4. Use classified ads to find jobs cleaning vehicles, such as at a car wash, car dealership, car rental business, or hotel with airport shuttle service. *Look for job openings for cleaning vehicles.*
5. Visit a car wash. Give the picture cards to the client. *Let's find someone who is using (a) _____.*
6. Have the clients wash staff cars or help them organize a car wash. Use the vocabulary words while giving the clients directions during the activity. *Get the _____. Use the _____.*

Word/Sentence Imitation and Sentence Completion
1. Ask the client to repeat each word after you say it. *Say _____.*
2. Use each word to complete the sentence *I use (a) _____.* Have the client repeat your sentences.
3. Print *I clean with (a) _____* on a card. Have the client complete the sentence using the vocabulary words.

Expressive Vocabulary
1. Name each picture.
2. What do all of these items have in common?
3. What do you do with a bucket?
4. What do you do with a chamois towel?
5. What do you do with window cleaner?
6. How do you use a hose to clean a vehicle?
7. How do you use a sponge to clean a vehicle?
8. How do you mix car wash detergent?
9. Name three kinds of vehicles you could clean.
10. (Cover the pictures.) If you were going to clean a vehicle, what would you need?

Expressive Activity
Have two clients role-play interviewing for a job washing vehicles. Have one client pretend to be the employer, and the other client can pretend to be the job applicant. Have them practice greeting each other, and ask the job applicant to use the vocabulary words to tell about himself, his job experiences, and why he wants the job.

Critical Thinking and Problem Solving
1. What should you pay attention to while rinsing a vehicle?
2. What would you do if the hose got pinched?
3. What do you do if the chamois towel gets too wet?
4. Why is it a good idea to rinse out the sponge often?
5. Why should you rinse the top of a vehicle first?
6. Why should you clean vehicles in a cool or shady place?
7. How can you tell where you have already washed?
8. How can you tell what part of a vehicle needs to be cleaned next?
9. Would you be interested in a job cleaning cars? Why?
10. If you were interviewing for a car cleaning job, what skills and experience would you say that you have?

Vocabulary During Leisure Activities: Amusement Park

Amusement Park

Receptive Vocabulary
Name each picture the client points to.

1. Point to the souvenir shop (roller coaster, tea cups, show, train, water ride).
2. Which has singing or dancing?
3. Which ride spins around?
4. Which ride zooms on water?
5. Which ride goes slowly on a track?
6. Which ride races around a track?
7. Where can you buy things?
8. Which would you see at an amusement park?
9. Which rides go fast? slow?
10. Which do you like?

Receptive Activities
Before doing these activities, make two copies of the picture grid. Cut apart one grid to make picture cards.

1. Give the client the picture grid. Have her match the picture cards to the pictures on the grid. *Where is/are the _____?*
2. Play a game of Bingo. Use pennies as markers.
3. Cover three to six pictures on the picture grid. Show the client a picture card and have her tell you where it was on the picture grid. *Where was/were the _____?*
4. Place the picture cards faceup on the table. Have the client follow your directions. *Touch the _____. Take the _____. Hand me the _____. Point to the _____. Turn over the _____.*
5. Look on amusement park websites. Locate rides and attractions that match the picture cards. *Find (a) _____.*
6. Visit an amusement park or a fair. Use the pictures to find the different rides and attractions. *Let's look for (a) _____.*

Word/Sentence Imitation and Sentence Completion
1. Ask the client to repeat each word after you say it. *Say _____.*
2. Use each word to complete the sentence *I see (a) _____.* Have the client repeat your sentences.
3. Print *The amusement park has (a) _____* on a card. Have the client complete the sentence using the vocabulary words.

Expressive Vocabulary
1. Name each picture.
2. Describe how to ride a roller coaster.
3. Name three things you might see in a show.
4. Tell what a water ride is like.
5. Describe a train ride.
6. Tell how to ride tea cups.
7. Name three items they sell at souvenir shops.
8. Name two amusement parks.
9. What do you like to do at an amusement park?
10. (Cover the pictures.) Name six things you could do at an amusement park.

Expressive Activity
Have the clients pretend they are at an amusement park. Encourage them to use the vocabulary words to talk about what they'll do first, second, etc.

Critical Thinking and Problem Solving
1. How could you make a plan to visit an amusement park with a friend?
2. Why is it a good idea to discuss the day, time, transportation, and permission before going to an amusement park with a friend?
3. How would you and a friend decide what to do first at an amusement park?
4. What if you and your friend like different rides?
5. Why do some people like roller coasters? Why do some people dislike roller coasters?
6. If a person doesn't like fast rides, what could she do at an amusement park?
7. What could happen if a person cuts in line for a ride?
8. Why is it a good idea to go on water rides when it is sunny?
9. What if you'd like to buy a $20 souvenir, but you only have $10?
10. What could you say to your friend if you had a good time with her at an amusement park?

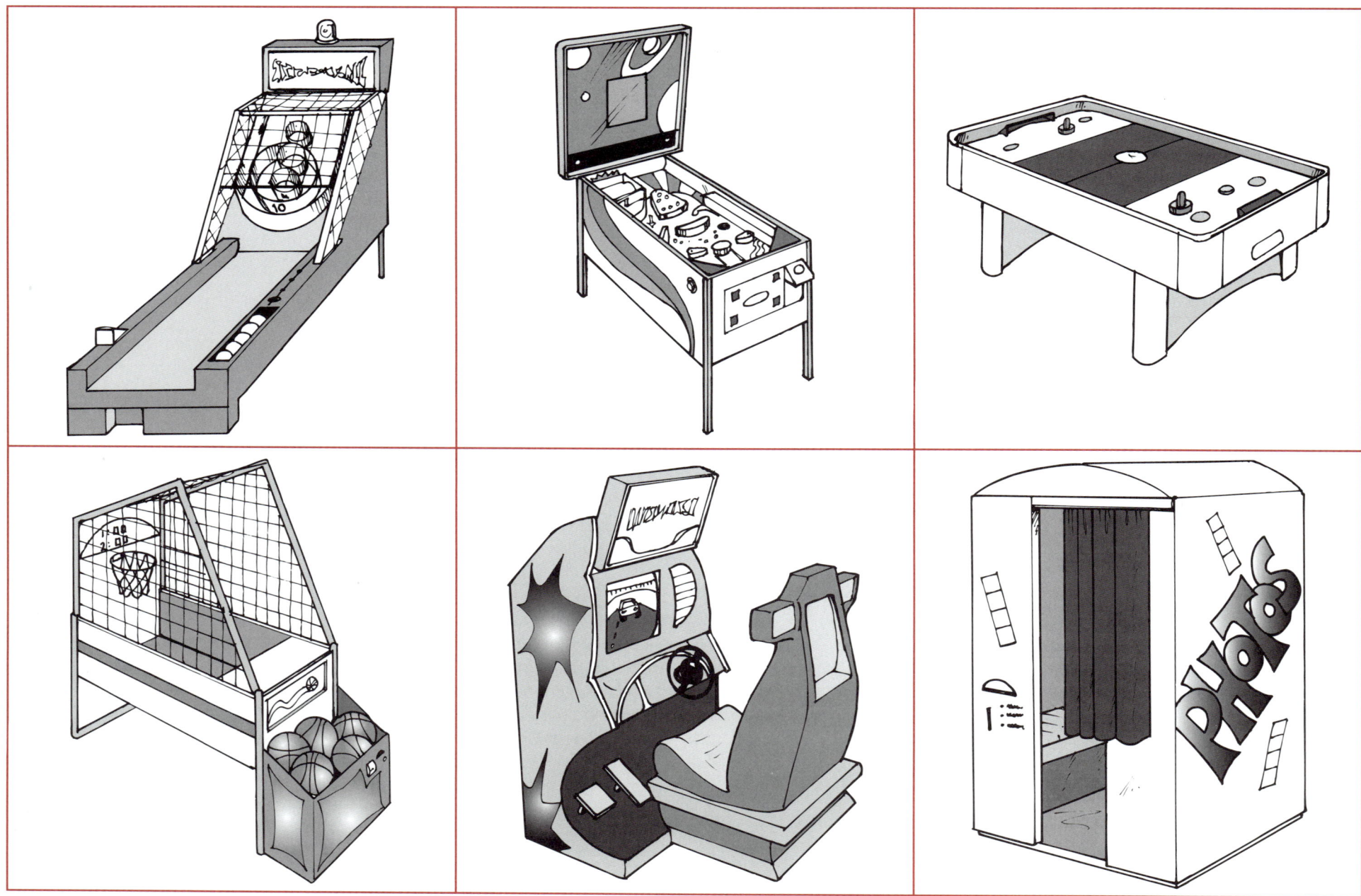

Vocabulary During Leisure Activities: Arcade

Arcade

Receptive Vocabulary
Name each picture the client points to.

1. Point to a pinball game (photo booth, Skee-Ball game, air hockey game, driving game, basketball game).
2. Which takes your picture?
3. Which game is like driving?
4. Which game do you hit a hockey puck?
5. Which game uses flippers and a silver ball?
6. Which game do you roll a ball up a ramp?
7. Which game do you shoot hoops?
8. Which cost money to play?
9. Which would you see at an arcade?
10. Which do you like to do?

Receptive Activities
Before doing these activities, make two copies of the picture grid. Cut apart one grid to make picture cards.

1. Give the client the picture grid. Have him match the picture cards to the pictures on the grid. *Where is the _____?*
2. Play a game of Bingo. Use pennies as markers.
3. Cover three to six pictures on the picture grid. Show the client a picture card and have him tell you where it was on the picture grid. *Where was the _____?*
4. Place the picture cards faceup on the table. Have the client follow your directions. *Touch the _____. Take the _____. Hand me the _____. Point to the _____. Turn over the _____.*
5. Look on arcade supplier websites. Find games and activities that match the picture cards. *Find a/an _____.*
6. Visit an arcade. Use the picture cards to find each activity. Try some. *Let's look for a/an _____.*

Word/Sentence Imitation and Sentence Completion
1. Ask the client to repeat each word after you say it. *Say _____.*
2. Use each word to complete the sentence *I like the _____.* Have the client repeat your sentences.
3. Print *My favorite is the _____* on a card. Have the client complete the sentence using the vocabulary words.

Expressive Vocabulary
1. Name each picture.
2. Describe how to play Skee-Ball.
3. Tell how to play a pinball game.
4. Explain how to play air hockey.
5. Describe how to play the basketball game.
6. Tell three arcade games.
7. Describe how to use the photo booth.
8. Where could you play arcade games?
9. Which games do you like to play? Why?
10. (Cover the pictures.) Name six things you could do at an arcade.

Expressive Activity
Have the client pretend that he's at an arcade with friends. Have him use the vocabulary words to talk about what he'd like to do first, second, etc.

Critical Thinking and Problem Solving
1. How could you make a plan to visit an arcade with a friend?
2. Why is it a good idea to discuss the day, time, transportation, and permission before going to an arcade with a friend?
3. How could you and a friend decide what game to play first?
4. What if you and your friend like different games?
5. What if your Skee-Ball goes off the ramp?
6. How do you earn the most tickets when playing Skee-Ball?
7. What if your flipper gets stuck on a pinball game?
8. What are some good strategies in air hockey?
9. What if you earn 50 tickets, but the prize you want costs 100 tickets?
10. What could you say to your friend if you had a good time with him at the arcade?

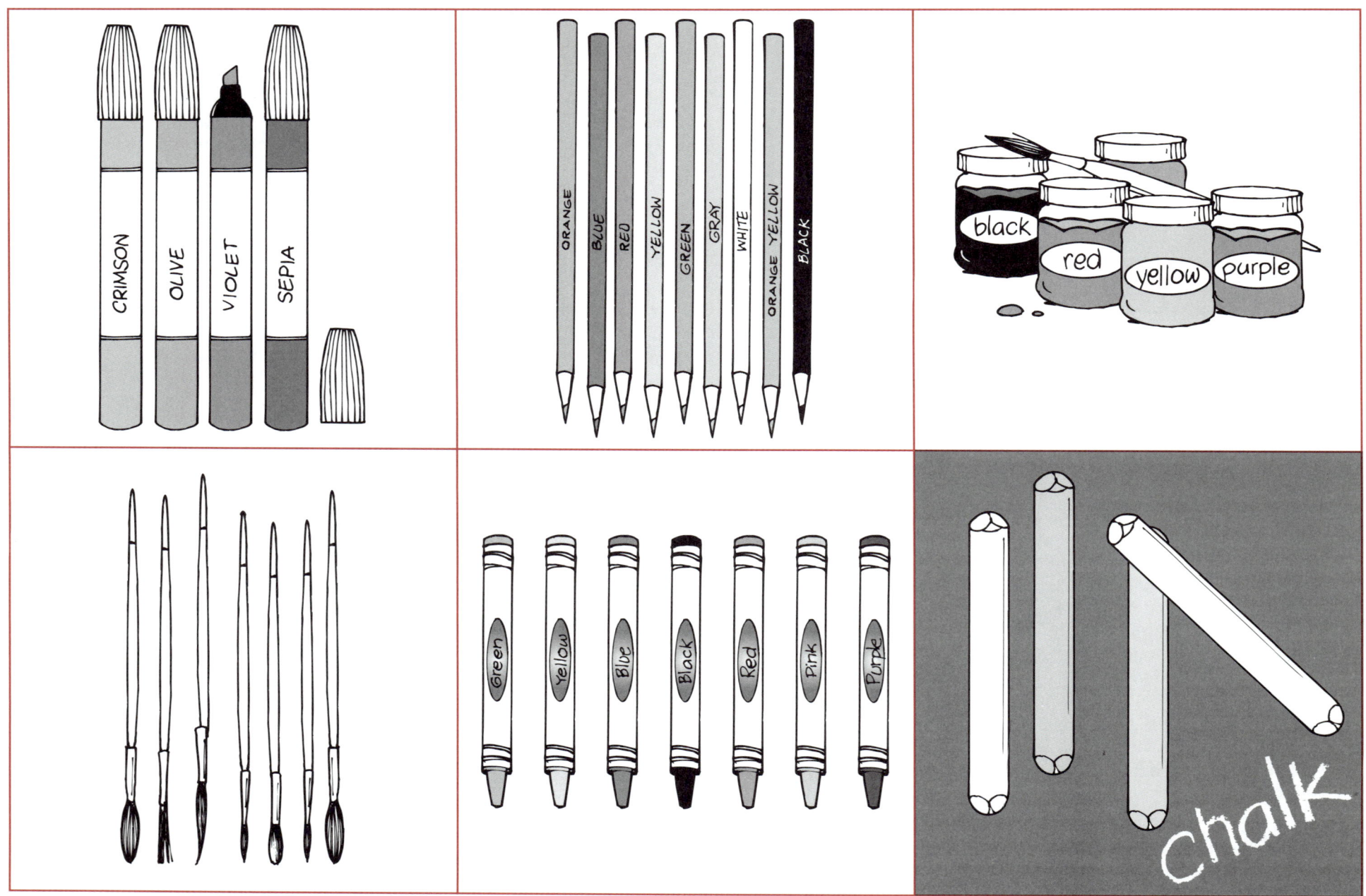

Vocabulary During Leisure Activities: Art

Art

Receptive Vocabulary
Name each picture the client points to.

1. Point to the colored pencils (paintbrushes, crayons, markers, watercolor paints, colored chalk).
2. Which do you use to paint?
3. Which can you draw with?
4. Which come in different colors?
5. Which get wet?
6. Which have lids?
7. Which can be used for art?
8. Which go on paper?
9. Which have you used?
10. Which do you like?

Receptive Activities
Before doing these activities, make two copies of the picture grid. Cut apart one grid to make picture cards.

1. Give the client the picture grid. Have her match the picture cards to the pictures on the grid. *Where is/are the _____?*
2. Play a game of Bingo. Use pennies as markers.
3. Place real markers, colored pencils, watercolor paints, etc., on the table. Give a picture card to the client and have her put it by the matching item. *Find the _____.*
4. Cover three to six pictures on the picture grid. Show the client a picture card and have her tell you where it was on the picture grid. *Where was/were the _____?*
5. Use ads from a local art store or a discount department store. *Find _____.*
6. Have the client draw or paint pictures using these items. Use the vocabulary to give the client directions to follow throughout the activity. *Get the colored pencils. Now use the colored chalk.*
7. Visit an art store or a department store. Use the pictures as a shopping list. *Let's look for _____.*

Word/Sentence Imitation and Sentence Completion
1. Ask the client to repeat each word after you say it. *Say _____.*
2. Use each word to complete the sentence *I use _____.* Have the client repeat your sentences.
3. Print *I need _____* on a card. Have the client complete the sentence using the vocabulary words.

Expressive Vocabulary
1. Name each picture.
2. What do all of these items have in common?
3. How are markers and colored pencils different?
4. Describe how to use watercolor paints and paintbrushes.
5. How are crayons and colored chalk different?
6. Describe how to trace a picture.
7. What do you like better, using coloring books or drawing freehand? Why?
8. Name three things you could draw.
9. Tell three places you could buy art supplies.
10. (Cover the pictures.) Name six art supplies that you could use to make a picture.

Expressive Activity
Have the client role-play asking a friend to draw or paint with her. Let her plan what materials she will need to do her art project. Encourage her to use the vocabulary words throughout the activity.

Critical Thinking and Problem Solving
1. What friends do you have who like to draw or paint?
2. How could you make a plan with a friend to do art together?
3. What supplies would you need if you wanted to draw?
4. What if you break the point on a colored pencil?
5. What if you spill your water while painting?
6. Why is it a good idea to put newspaper on the table when painting?
7. What could you do with a picture you paint that is still wet?
8. What if you and your friend want to use the same colored marker at the same time?
9. What can you do with the pictures you make?
10. What could you say to your friend if you had a good time doing art with her?

Vocabulary During Leisure Activities: Baseball
Functional Vocabulary for Adolescents & Adults

Baseball

Receptive Vocabulary
Name each picture the client points to.

1. Point to (the) mitt (bat, baseball, hit, strike, run).
2. Which ball is used in baseball?
3. Which protects your hand?
4. Which do you hit the ball with?
5. What is it called if your bat misses the ball?
6. What is it called when the bat connects with the ball?
7. How do you get to first base?
8. Which do you see at a baseball game?
9. Which do you need to play baseball?
10. Which are things a batter could do?

Receptive Activities
Before doing these activities, make two copies of the picture grid. Cut apart one grid to make picture cards.

1. Give the client the picture grid. Have him match the picture cards to the pictures on the grid. *Where is the _____?*
2. Play a game of Bingo. Use pennies as markers.
3. Play a game of baseball. You may modify the game by using a T-ball stand, a large plastic bat, and a Wiffle® ball or a beach ball. Use the vocabulary words during the game. *Get the bat. Put on your mitt. You scored a run!*
4. Look for a baseball field at your school or at a nearby park, and watch a PE class or teams play a game. Or watch a video of a baseball game. Give the client the picture cards and have him note the equipment and actions that match the vocabulary words.
5. Use ads from a local toy store or a sporting goods store. Find baseballs, bats, mitts, and other baseball equipment. *Find (a/an) _____.*
6. Visit a toy store or a sporting goods store. Look for baseball equipment. *Let's look for (a/an) _____.*

Word/Sentence Imitation and Sentence Completion
1. Ask the client to repeat each word after you say it. *Say _____.*
2. Use each word to complete the sentence *I see (a) _____.* Have the client repeat your sentences.
3. Print *Get a _____* on a card. Have the client complete the sentence using the vocabulary words.

Expressive Vocabulary
1. Name each picture.
2. What do all of these items and actions have in common?
3. Why do baseball players wear mitts?
4. Name three actions you can do with a baseball in a game.
5. What do you do with a bat?
6. What happens after three strikes?
7. What happens after you hit the ball?
8. Name a professional baseball team.
9. Tell three positions in baseball.
10. Describe how to play the game of baseball.

Expressive Activity
Have the client role-play asking some friends to watch a professional baseball game. Instruct him to tell his friends where they will watch the game, what day and time to come, and to get permission. They should also talk about transportation and discuss how much money to bring.

Critical Thinking and Problem Solving
1. If you were to play baseball, what equipment would you need to bring?
2. Why is it a good idea to cheer for your friends when they are up to bat?
3. Why is it a good idea to know when it is your turn to bat?
4. If you hit the ball, why is it a good idea to set the bat down before running to base rather than throw it?
5. How do you know which base to run to?
6. When running to a base, how could you be a good sport if you get tagged out?
7. When playing outfield, why is it a good idea to pay attention to the game?
8. How could you plan to go to a professional baseball game with a friend?
9. How would you act if your favorite team won the game?
10. How would you act if your favorite team lost the game?

Basketball

Receptive Vocabulary
Name each picture the client points to.

1. Point to basket/hoop (dribble, jump ball, three-point shot, rebound, free throw).
2. Which does the ball go in?
3. Who is bouncing the ball?
4. Who is shooting from the foul line?
5. Who is getting the ball after a basket?
6. Which is making a basket from behind the three-point line?
7. Which shows two players jumping for a ball to start the game?
8. Which would you see at a basketball game?
9. Which score points?
10. Which are actions?

Receptive Activities
Before doing these activities, make two copies of the picture grid. Cut apart one grid to make picture cards.

1. Give the client the picture grid. Have her match the picture cards to the pictures on the grid. *Where is the _____?*
2. Play a game of Bingo. Use pennies as markers.
3. Let the clients play a game of basketball. You may modify the game by using trash cans for hoops, a beach ball, and chalk or tape to mark the court. Use vocabulary words during the game. *Let's start with a jump ball. Dribble the ball. Try to shoot a three-point shot.*
4. Look for basketball courts at your school or at a nearby park, and watch a PE class or teams play a game. Or watch a video of a basketball game. Give the client the picture cards and have her note the equipment and actions that match the vocabulary words.
5. Use ads from a local toy store or a sporting goods store, or visit a toy store or a sporting goods store. *Find a basketball and a basketball hoop.*
6. Look at photos on a website for the NBA or basketball team. Look at action shots of players. *Find someone who is _____.*

Word/Sentence Imitation and Sentence Completion
1. Ask the client to repeat each word after you say it. *Say _____.*
2. Use each word to complete the sentence *There is a _____.* Have the client repeat your sentences.
3. Print *I see a _____* on a card. Have the client complete the sentence using the vocabulary words.

Expressive Vocabulary
1. Name each picture.
2. What do all of these items and actions have in common?
3. Describe the basket.
4. How is a jump ball done?
5. What is a rebound?
6. What is a free throw?
7. Describe a three-point shot.
8. What is dribbling?
9. Describe how to play basketball.
10. (Cover the pictures.) Name six items and actions you'd see at a basketball game.

Expressive Activity
Let the clients play a game of basketball. You may modify the game by using trash cans for hoops, a beach ball, and chalk or tape to mark the court. Have the clients use the vocabulary words to describe what's happening throughout the activity.

Critical Thinking and Problem Solving
1. At the beginning of the basketball game, how do the officials decide which team will get the ball?
2. How do you know which basket is for your team?
3. What happens if someone fouls?
4. How do players play defense?
5. How do players play offense?
6. Why is it a good idea to pay attention to the ball during the game?
7. What should you do when you get the ball?
8. What should you do if the referee calls a foul on you?
9. How does a good sport act when she's losing the game? winning?
10. Do you like basketball? Why?

Birthday Party

Receptive Vocabulary
Name each picture the client points to.

1. Point to the present (invitation, cake, candles, balloon, RSVP).
2. Which is a round decoration?
3. Which card invites you to a party?
4. How do you let someone know if you can come to the party?
5. Which food has frosting?
6. Which does the birthday person blow out?
7. Which do you give to the birthday person?
8. Which have you seen at a birthday party?
9. Which could you buy at a party supply store?
10. Which do you want for your birthday?

Receptive Activities
Before doing these activities, make two copies of the picture grid. Cut apart one grid to make picture cards.

1. Give the client the picture grid. Have him match the picture cards to the pictures on the grid. *Where is/are the _____?*
2. Play a game of Bingo. Use pennies as markers.
3. Place a real present, invitation, RSVP message, etc., on the table. Give a picture card to the client and have him put it by the matching item. *Find the _____.*
4. Place the picture cards faceup on the table. Have the client follow your directions. *Touch the _____. Take the _____. Hand me the _____. Point to the _____. Turn over the _____.*
5. Cover three to six pictures on the picture grid. Show the client a picture card and have him tell you where it was on the picture grid. *Where was/were the _____?*
6. Use ads from a party supply store or a drug store. *Find (a/an) _____.*
7. Visit a party supply store. Use the pictures as a shopping list. *Let's look for (a/an) _____.*

Word/Sentence Imitation and Sentence Completion
1. Ask the client to repeat each word after you say it. *Say _____.*
2. Use each word to complete the sentence *Get the _____.* Have the client repeat your sentences.
3. Print *I see (a/an) _____* on a card. Have the client complete the sentence using the vocabulary words.

Expressive Vocabulary
1. Name each picture.
2. What do all of these items have in common?
3. What information is on an invitation?
4. What does it mean to RSVP?
5. What are three gift ideas for a friend?
6. How do you blow up a balloon?
7. What are three flavors of cake?
8. What happens if the birthday person blows out all the candles?
9. Describe your favorite birthday party.
10. (Cover the pictures.) Name four items you could see at a birthday party.

Expressive Activity
Plan a birthday party (real or pretend). Have the client discuss what to put on the invitation and what supplies to buy for the party.

Critical Thinking and Problem Solving
1. How do you decide when to have your birthday party?
2. How do you decide who to invite to your birthday party?
3. Why is it a good idea to have people RSVP to your party?
4. What decorations would you like at your party?
5. What food would you like to serve at your party?
6. Where could you buy your party supplies?
7. What games or entertainment would you like at your party?
8. What if you open a present and you don't like it? What if it's the wrong size?
9. What would be a nice thing to say to people who give you presents?
10. What could you say to friends at the end of your birthday party?

Vocabulary During Leisure Activities: Board Games
Functional Vocabulary for Adolescents & Adults

Board Games

Receptive Vocabulary
Name each picture the client points to.

1. Point to the dice (game board, start, spinner, game piece, draw pile).
2. Which do you put your game pieces on?
3. Which do you roll?
4. Which do you spin?
5. Which marker do you move?
6. Which cards do you pick up?
7. Where do you begin the game?
8. Which can have words on it?
9. Which would you see in a board game?
10. Which have you used in a board game?

Receptive Activities
Before doing these activities, make two copies of the picture grid. Cut apart one grid to make picture cards.

1. Give the client the picture grid. Have her match the picture cards to the pictures on the grid. *Where is/are the _____?*
2. Play a game of Bingo. Use pennies as markers.
3. Place a real board game on the table. Give a picture card to the client and have her put it by the matching item. *Find the _____.*
4. Place the picture cards faceup on the table. Have the client follow your directions. *Touch the _____. Take the _____. Hand me the _____. Point to the _____. Turn over the _____.*
5. Cover three to six pictures on the picture grid. Show the client a picture card and have her tell you where it was on the picture grid. *Where was/were the _____?*
6. Use ads from a local sporting goods store. *Find a _____.*
7. Play a board game. Use the vocabulary words to give the clients directions to follow during the game.
8. Visit a toy store or a discount department store and look at the board games. *Let's look for a game that has (a) _____.*

Word/Sentence Imitation and Sentence Completion
1. Ask the client to repeat each word after you say it. *Say _____.*
2. Use each word to complete the sentence *Here is/are the _____.* Have the client repeat your sentences.
3. Print *I found the _____* on a card. Have the client complete the sentence using the vocabulary words.

Expressive Vocabulary
1. Name each picture.
2. What do all of these items have in common?
3. What do you do with a spinner?
4. What do you do with the dice?
5. What do you do with a game piece?
6. What is on the game board?
7. What do you do with a draw pile?
8. Name three board games.
9. Describe how to play a board game.
10. (Cover the pictures.) Name six parts of a board game.

Expressive Activity
Play a board game. Have the client use the vocabulary words to request the items she needs and to describe what each person is doing on her turn.

Critical Thinking and Problem Solving
1. How could you ask a friend if he'd like to play a game?
2. How would you two decide which game to play?
3. What would you do if you wanted to buy a new game?
4. How do you decide who gets which color game piece?
5. How do you decide who goes first?
6. How do you know how far to move on your turn?
7. What if you roll the dice, but they fall on the floor?
8. Why is it a good idea to pay attention when it is your turn?
9. How does a good sport act when she is losing? winning?
10. If you had fun playing the game, what could you say to your friend?

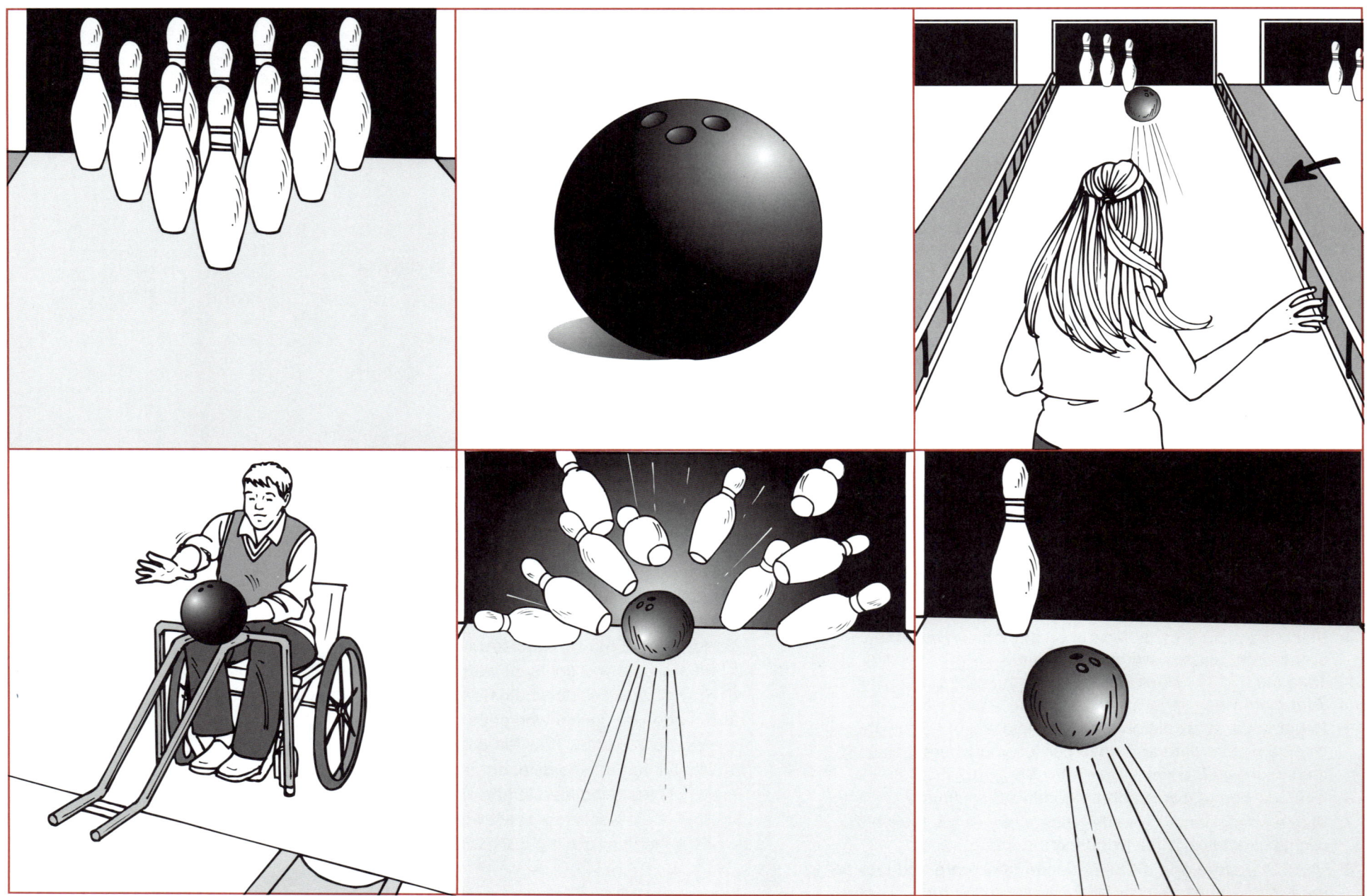

Vocabulary During Leisure Activities: Bowling

Bowling

Receptive Vocabulary
Name each picture the client points to.

1. Point to the pins (bumpers, bowling ball, ramp, strike, spare).
2. Which ball do you bowl with?
3. Which do you knock down?
4. Which keep the balls in the lane?
5. Which means that you knocked all the pins down with one ball?
6. Which means that you knocked all the pins down with two balls?
7. Which helps people get the ball started rolling down the lane?
8. Which would you see at a bowling alley?
9. Which gives you an X on the score sheet?
10. Which gives you a / on the score sheet?

Receptive Activities
Before doing these activities, make two copies of the picture grid. Cut apart one grid to make picture cards.

1. Give the client the picture grid. Have him match the picture cards to the pictures on the grid. *Where is/are the _____?*
2. Play a game of Bingo. Use pennies as markers.
3. Cover three to six pictures on the picture grid. Show the client a picture card and have him tell you where it was on the picture grid. *Where was/were the _____?*
4. Place the picture cards faceup on the table. Have the client follow your directions. *Touch the _____. Take the _____. Hand me the _____. Point to the _____. Turn over the _____.*
5. Play a bowling game using ten empty two-liter bottles and a playground ball. Use the pictures and bowling vocabulary during the game.
6. Go bowling at a bowling alley. Use the pictures and vocabulary during the activity.

Word/Sentence Imitation and Sentence Completion
1. Ask the client to repeat each word after you say it. *Say _____.*
2. Use each word to complete the sentence *I see (a) _____.* Have the client repeat your sentences.
3. Print *Get the _____* on a card. Have the client complete the sentence using the vocabulary words.

Expressive Vocabulary
1. Name each picture.
2. What do all of these items have in common?
3. What do you try to do with the pins?
4. How do you roll the bowling ball?
5. What do the bumpers do?
6. What does the ramp do?
7. What is a strike?
8. What is a spare?
9. Where could you go bowling?
10. (Cover the pictures.) Name six things you could see at a bowling alley.

Expressive Activity
Practice bowling, either at a bowling alley or using ten empty two-liter bottles and a playground ball. Ask the clients to use the vocabulary words to describe what they are doing during the game.

Critical Thinking and Problem Solving
1. How could you make a plan to go bowling with a friend?
2. When renting bowling shoes, how can you find out your shoe size?
3. How do you decide if you need bumpers or a ramp? How would you ask for them?
4. What do you consider when choosing a bowling ball?
5. Why is it a good idea to know when it's your turn?
6. What strategies do you use when rolling the bowling ball?
7. What if the pins aren't reset for your turn?
8. How is the score kept when you get a strike?
9. How is the score kept when you get a spare?
10. If you had fun bowling with your friend, what could you say to her?

Vocabulary During Leisure Activities: Camping

Camping

Receptive Vocabulary
Name each picture the client points to.

1. Point to the water bottle (tent, campfire, lantern, sleeping pad, sleeping bag).
2. Which is like a small home?
3. Which do you sleep in?
4. Which goes under the sleeping bag?
5. Which do you roast marshmallows over?
6. Which lights the area at night?
7. Which holds drinking water?
8. Which would you see at a campout?
9. Which would you pack for a campout?
10. Which have you used before?

Receptive Activities
Before doing these activities, make two copies of the picture grid. Cut apart one grid to make picture cards.

1. Give the client the picture grid. Have her match the picture cards to the pictures on the grid. *Where is the _____?*
2. Cover three to six pictures on the picture grid. Show the client a picture card and have her tell you where it was on the picture grid. *Where was the _____?*
3. Place the picture cards faceup on the table. Have the client follow your directions. *Touch the _____. Take the _____. Hand me the _____. Point to the _____. Turn over the _____.*
4. Pitch a tent, unroll a sleeping bag, and pretend to have a campout. Give the client directions throughout the activity. *Fill the water bottle. Put the sleeping bag on top of the pad. Get the lantern.*
5. Use ads from a local sporting goods store or look on a website that contains camping gear. *Find (a/an) _____.*
6. Visit the camping section of a sporting goods store. Use the pictures as a shopping list. *Let's look for a _____.*
7. Go to a campground. Give the client the picture cards and ask her to find these items. *Find a _____.*

Word/Sentence Imitation and Sentence Completion
1. Ask the client to repeat each word after you say it. *Say _____.*
2. Use each word to complete the sentence *Pack the _____.* Have the client repeat your sentences.
3. Print *I see the _____* on a card. Have the client complete the sentence using the vocabulary words.

Expressive Vocabulary
1. Name each picture.
2. What do all of these items have in common?
3. What do you do with a tent?
4. What do you do with a lantern?
5. What do you do with a sleeping bag?
6. What do you do with a sleeping pad?
7. What do you do with a water bottle?
8. What do you do at a campfire?
9. What would you pack for a campout?
10. (Cover the pictures.) Name six items you would see at a campout.

Expressive Activity
Have the client role-play planning a campout. Encourage her to discuss which days and times to go, the camping location, transportation she'll need to get to the campground, and permission she might need. Have her talk about what she should pack and what the meal menus will be.

Critical Thinking and Problem Solving
1. Why is it a good idea to check the weather when packing for a camping trip?
2. Why is it a good idea to bring plenty of drinking water on a camping trip?
3. What could you help with when setting up camp?
4. Why is it a good idea to stake down the tent?
5. What are some safety rules for standing around the campfire?
6. What would you do if you roast a marshmallow and it catches on fire?
7. While hiking, why is it a good idea to stay with the group?
8. Why shouldn't you feed wild animals?
9. Why shouldn't you keep food in your tent?
10. Do you like camping? Why?

Vocabulary During Leisure Activities: Carnival
Functional Vocabulary for Adolescents & Adults

Carnival

Receptive Vocabulary
Name each picture the client points to.

1. Point to the Ferris wheel (giant slide, Tilt-a-Whirl, bumper cars, merry-go-round/carousel, Zipper).
2. Which spin around fast?
3. Which whirls and goes high?
4. Which do you drive?
5. Which slowly goes high?
6. Which has pretend horses?
7. Which do you slide down?
8. Which are at a carnival?
9. Which have you gone on?
10. Which do you like?

Receptive Activities
Before doing these activities, make two copies of the picture grid. Cut apart one grid to make picture cards.

1. Give the client the picture grid. Have him match the picture cards to the pictures on the grid. *Where is/are the _____?*
2. Play a game of Bingo. Use pennies as markers.
3. Cover three to six pictures on the picture grid. Show the client a picture card and have him tell you where it was on the picture grid. *Where was/were the _____?*
4. Place the picture cards faceup on the table. Have the client follow your directions. *Touch the _____. Take the _____. Hand me the _____. Point to the _____. Turn over the _____.*
5. Find a carnival ride website by typing "carnival rides" on an Internet search engine. Find rides that match the picture cards. *Find (a) _____.*
6. Visit a local fair or carnival. Use the picture cards to choose activities to do while at the event. *Let's ride on the _____.*

Word/Sentence Imitation and Sentence Completion
1. Ask the client to repeat each word after you say it. *Say _____.*
2. Use each word to complete the sentence *I ride the _____.* Have the client repeat your sentences.
3. Print *Let's watch the _____* on a card. Have the client complete the sentence using the vocabulary words.

Expressive Vocabulary
1. Name each picture.
2. What do all of these items have in common?
3. Describe the Ferris wheel.
4. How do you ride a merry-go-round?
5. What do you do on a giant slide?
6. What do you do on a Tilt-a-Whirl?
7. What does the Zipper do?
8. What do you do on bumper cars?
9. Which do you like to ride on? Why?
10. (Cover the pictures.) Name six carnival rides.

Expressive Activity
Let the client role-play planning a trip to a fair or a carnival. He can practice asking his friends to go and discussing the date, time, how they'll get there, how much money they should bring, and getting permission.

Critical Thinking and Problem Solving
1. How can you find out when a carnival is in town?
2. How could you invite some friends to the carnival? What should you talk about to plan the trip?
3. What happens if you get out of line when buying tickets?
4. How do you and your friends decide which rides to go on next?
5. How can you find out where the different rides are?
6. What if your friends like to go on different rides than you do?
7. What could you do if you feel sick after a ride?
8. What if you'd like a snack, but you only have a little bit of money?
9. What if you get lost at the carnival?
10. If you had a good time with your friends at a carnival, what could you say to them?

Vocabulary During Leisure Activities: Crafts

Crafts

Receptive Vocabulary
Name each picture the client points to.

1. Point to the beads (stickers, clay, rubber stamps, glue, glitter).
2. Which makes things stick together?
3. Which is sparkly?
4. Which are pictures that stick to paper?
5. Which can you mold into shapes?
6. Which can make a necklace?
7. Which puts ink on paper?
8. Which could you use to decorate cards?
9. Which have you used?
10. Which would you like to use?

Receptive Activities
Before doing these activities, make two copies of the picture grid. Cut apart one grid to make picture cards.

1. Give the client the picture grid. Have her match the picture cards to the pictures on the grid. *Where is/are the _____?*
2. Play a game of Bingo. Use pennies as markers.
3. Place real clay, beads, glue, glitter, etc., on the table. Give a picture card to the client and have her put it by the matching item. *Find the _____.*
4. Make a craft item using some of these materials. Use the vocabulary words to give the client directions to follow throughout the activity. *Squirt glue on the paper. Sprinkle glitter on the glue. Decorate your project with stickers.*
5. Cover three to six pictures on the picture grid. Show the client a picture card and have her tell you where it was on the picture grid. *Where was/were the _____?*
6. Use ads from a craft store or a discount department store. *Find _____.*
7. Visit a craft store or a discount department store. Use the pictures as a shopping list. *Let's look for _____.*

Word/Sentence Imitation and Sentence Completion
1. Ask the client to repeat each word after you say it. *Say _____.*
2. Use each word to complete the sentence *I use _____.* Have the client repeat your sentences.
3. Print *I make it with _____* on a card. Have the client complete the sentence using the vocabulary words.

Expressive Vocabulary
1. Name each picture.
2. What do all of these items have in common?
3. Name three things you could make with clay.
4. Describe how to make a bead necklace.
5. Tell three things you could glue together.
6. Explain how to put glitter on something.
7. Describe how to use rubber stamps to make cards.
8. Tell three things that could be pictured on stickers.
9. Where could you buy craft supplies?
10. (Cover the pictures.) Name six craft supplies.

Expressive Activity
Have the clients role-play planning a craft project. You can search the Internet for craft ideas that pertain to the upcoming holiday or theme for your classroom. Have your clients plan what to make, decide what materials they'll need, determine what materials need to be purchased, and make a shopping list.

Critical Thinking and Problem Solving
1. What can you do to keep your clothes clean while using clay?
2. How can you organize your beads so they don't spill on the floor?
3. What do you do if the glue doesn't pour from the bottle?
4. When using glitter, how can you save the extra glitter that doesn't stick to your project?
5. Why is it a good idea to get enough ink on your rubber stamp before stamping?
6. Why is it a good idea to know where you want to put a sticker before placing it on the paper?
7. Where can you get craft project ideas?
8. How could you invite a friend to do crafts with you?
9. What would you need to do to plan for the craft activity?
10. If you had a good time doing crafts with a friend, what could you tell him?

Dance

Receptive Vocabulary
Name each picture the client points to.

1. Point to the band (deejay, prom, refreshments, corsage, boutonniere).
2. Which shows a formal dance?
3. Which are the food and drinks?
4. Who is playing musical instruments?
5. Who is playing CDs?
6. Which flower is for a guy?
7. Which flowers are for a girl?
8. Which would you see at a formal dance?
9. What could you see at a casual dance?
10. Which have you seen before?

Receptive Activities
Before doing these activities, make two copies of the picture grid. Cut apart one grid to make picture cards.

1. Give the client the picture grid. Have him match the picture cards to the pictures on the grid. *Where is/are the _____?*
2. Play a game of Bingo. Use pennies as markers.
3. Cover three to six pictures on the picture grid. Show the client a picture card and have him tell you where it was on the picture grid. *Where was/were the _____?*
4. Place the picture cards faceup on the table. Have the client follow your directions. *Touch the _____. Take the _____. Hand me the _____. Point to the _____. Turn over the _____.*
5. Look at grocery store ads or in a cookbook with many pictures. Find items that would be good refreshments to serve at a dance. *Let's find some refreshments.*
6. Visit a florist shop or find pictures on a floral website by typing "corsage" or "boutonniere" on the images feature of an Internet search engine. Look at the samples or pictures. *Find a corsage. Find a boutonniere.*
7. Search for "deejay" and "band" using the images feature of an Internet search engine. *Find a band. Find a deejay.*

Word/Sentence Imitation and Sentence Completion
1. Ask the client to repeat each word after you say it. *Say _____.*
2. Use each word to complete the sentence *Here is/are (a) _____.* Have the client repeat your sentences.
3. Print *I see (a) _____* on a card. Have the client complete the sentence using the vocabulary words.

Expressive Vocabulary
1. Name each picture.
2. What do all of these people and items have in common?
3. What is a prom?
4. What is a corsage?
5. What is a boutonniere?
6. What are refreshments?
7. What does a deejay do?
8. What does a band do?
9. Which do you like better, a deejay or a band? Why?
10. (Cover the pictures.) What dances do you know about?

Expressive Activity
Have the client role-play taking someone to a dance. He can practice asking the person out, buying flowers, dancing to fast music, slow dancing with a partner, and using manners while having refreshments.

Critical Thinking and Problem Solving
1. How do you find out if there is a dance coming up?
2. What would you do if you wanted to go to a formal dance with someone?
3. What kind of clothes do people wear to a prom? How do they get those clothes?
4. What flower arrangements do people buy for the prom? How do they buy them?
5. What kind of clothes do people wear to an informal dance?
6. What is the difference between a prom and an informal dance?
7. Which do you like better, a prom or an informal dance? Why?
8. What are some manners you should use while getting refreshments?
9. How do you have fun at a dance?
10. If you had a good time at a dance, what could you tell your friends or your date?

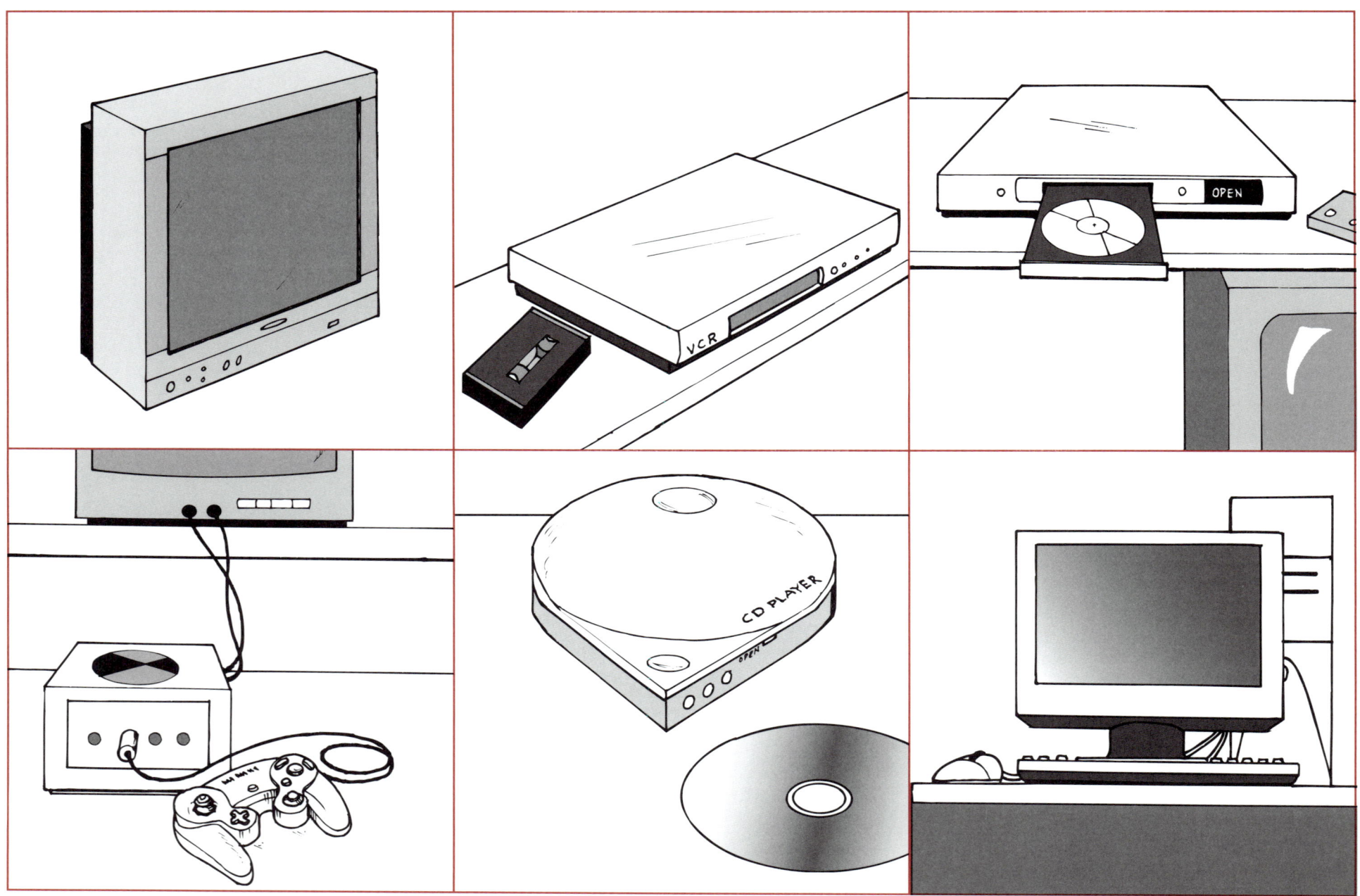

Electronic Entertainment

Receptive Vocabulary
Name each picture the client points to.

1. Point to the computer (VCR, CD player, DVD player, TV, video game system).
2. Which play music?
3. Which have games?
4. Which show movies?
5. Which has television shows?
6. Which has the Internet?
7. Which take CDs?
8. Which can you carry?
9. Which are plugged in?
10. Which do you like?

Receptive Activities
Before doing these activities, make two copies of the picture grid. Cut apart one grid to make picture cards.

1. Give the client the picture grid. Have her match the picture cards to the pictures on the grid. *Where is the _____?*
2. Play a game of Bingo. Use pennies as markers.
3. Go to a room that has a real computer, VCR, TV, etc., in it. Give a picture card to the client and have her put it by the matching item. *Find the _____.*
4. Place a TV remote, CD, DVD, videotape, video game system, and computer disc on the table. Have the client match these items to the electronic devices they go with, either real items in the room or the picture cards. *Which goes with a _____?*
5. Cover three to six pictures on the picture grid. Show the client a picture card and have her tell you where it was on the picture grid. *Where was the _____?*
6. Use ads from an electronics store, or visit an electronics store or a video rental store. Use the pictures as a shopping list. *Let's look for a _____.*

Word/Sentence Imitation and Sentence Completion
1. Ask the client to repeat each word after you say it. *Say _____.*
2. Use each word to complete the sentence *I use a _____.* Have the client repeat your sentences.
3. Print *Turn on the _____* on a card. Have the client complete the sentence using the vocabulary words.

Expressive Vocabulary
1. Name each picture.
2. What do all of these items have in common?
3. Name three TV shows that you like.
4. Tell three movies you could watch on VCR or DVD.
5. What video games do you like?
6. What music do you like?
7. What are three things you can do on the computer?
8. How are a videotape and a DVD different?
9. How are a CD player and a portable CD player different?
10. (Cover the pictures.) Name six forms of electronic entertainment.

Expressive Activity
Have the client role-play planning to get together with a friend to use one of these electronic forms of entertainment. They can plan the activity, including what they would like to do, when they will do it, where they will do it, transportation, and getting permission. They can discuss what TV show or movie they'd like to see, what music they'd like to listen to, or what video game they'd like to play.

Critical Thinking and Problem Solving
1. How do you find out what TV shows are on and what channels they are on?
2. How would you decide whether to rent or to buy a DVD?
3. How are the DVDs and videotapes organized at your video store?
4. How do you find the movie that you like?
5. What if you and your friend like different video games?
6. When playing video games, why is it a good idea to let your friend play too?
7. How is your music store organized?
8. How do you find the CD that you like?
9. Why is it a good idea to take off your headphones when crossing a street?
10. What are some safety rules about sharing personal information on the Internet?

Vocabulary During Leisure Activities: Football

Football

Receptive Vocabulary
Name each picture the client points to.

1. Point to the yard line (goalpost, kick off, touchdown, pass, punt).
2. Which is a post at both ends of a football field?
3. Which stripe marks distances on a football field?
4. Who is throwing?
5. Who is kicking?
6. Which one starts the game?
7. Which is scoring six points?
8. Which two are parts of a football field?
9. Which are football plays?
10. Which have you done?

Receptive Activities
Before doing these activities, make two copies of the picture grid. Cut apart one grid to make picture cards.

1. Give the client the picture grid. Have him match the picture cards to the pictures on the grid. *Where is the _____?*
2. Play a game of Bingo. Use pennies as markers.
3. Look for the football field at your school. Watch a PE class play a game. Use the vocabulary words to talk about the field and the game while you're watching it.
4. Place the picture cards faceup on the table. Have the client follow your directions. *Touch the _____. Take the _____. Hand me the _____. Point to the _____. Turn over the _____.*
5. Type the vocabulary words on the images feature of an Internet search engine. *Find the _____.*
6. Watch a video of a football game. Note the parts of the field and the actions that match the vocabulary words. *There's a _____.*
7. Play a game of football. You may modify the game by playing flag football and using a Nerf football. Use the vocabulary words during the game. *Let's line up on the 10-yard line. It's your turn to punt. Let's pass this one.*

Word/Sentence Imitation and Sentence Completion
1. Ask the client to repeat each word after you say it. *Say _____.*
2. Use each word to complete the sentence *Here is a _____.* Have the client repeat your sentences.
3. Print *This is a _____* on a card. Have the client complete the sentence using the vocabulary words.

Expressive Vocabulary
1. Name each picture.
2. What do all of these items and actions have in common?
3. What happens at the goalposts?
4. What are the yard lines?
5. What is a kick off?
6. What is a pass?
7. What is a punt?
8. What is a touchdown?
9. Name three football teams.
10. (Cover the pictures.) Name six items and actions you'd see at a football game.

Expressive Activity
Let the clients play a game of football. You may modify the game by playing flag football and using a Nerf football. Have the clients use the vocabulary words during the game.

Critical Thinking and Problem Solving
1. How could you make a plan to watch a football game with a friend?
2. How do you know which goalpost is the goal for your team?
3. Why is it a good idea to listen to the play before playing?
4. Why is it a good idea to pay attention to the ball during the game?
5. How do you know where to throw the ball?
6. How do you know which direction to run?
7. What if a player from the other team gets you?
8. What does a good sport do when he loses? wins?
9. Do you like football? Why?
10. Which do you like better, watching football or playing football? Why?

Fun Choices

Receptive Vocabulary
Name each picture the client points to.

1. Point to the cards (dominoes, puzzle, board game, Frisbee, bingo).
2. Which game has dice?
3. Which game is dealt?
4. Which can you throw?
5. Which do you match dots?
6. Which has pieces that make a picture?
7. Which is a game with numbers and letters?
8. Which can be played inside?
9. Which should be played outside?
10. Which do you like to play?

Receptive Activities
Before doing these activities, make two copies of the picture grid. Cut apart one grid to make picture cards.

1. Give the client the picture grid. Have her match the picture cards to the pictures on the grid. *Where is/are the _____?*
2. Play a game of Bingo. Use pennies as markers.
3. Place a real puzzle, board game, deck of cards, etc., on the table. Give a picture card to the client and have her put it by the matching item. *Find the _____.*
4. Place the picture cards faceup on the table. Have the client follow your directions. *Touch the _____. Take the _____. Hand me the _____. Point to the _____. Turn over the _____.*
5. Play a board game, a card game, dominoes or a game of bingo. Put together a puzzle. Play with a Frisbee. Use the vocabulary words while doing these activities.
6. Use ads from a local toy store or a discount department store. *Find (a/an) _____.*
7. Visit a toy store or a discount department store. Use the pictures as a shopping list. *Let's look for (a) _____.*

Word/Sentence Imitation and Sentence Completion
1. Ask the client to repeat each word after you say it. *Say _____.*
2. Use each word to complete the sentence *I play with (a) _____.* Have the client repeat your sentences.
3. Print *Let's play (a) _____* on a card. Have the client complete the sentence using the vocabulary words.

Expressive Vocabulary
1. Name each picture.
2. What do all of these things have in common?
3. What do you do with puzzle pieces?
4. How do you play a board game?
5. What can you play with cards?
6. How do you play bingo?
7. How do you play dominoes?
8. What do you do with a Frisbee?
9. Which of these to you like to do?
10. (Cover the pictures.) Name six fun things to do.

Expressive Activity
Let the client role-play asking a friend to play a game. The clients can use the vocabulary words to discuss their choices. They can then decide what game they would like to play and agree upon the rules.

Critical Thinking and Problem Solving
1. What strategies do you use to put a puzzle together?
2. How do you decide who goes first in a board game?
3. Why is it a good idea to know when it's your turn?
4. What do you do if you don't understand how to play a card game?
5. What could happen if you don't pay attention during a game of bingo?
6. Why is it a good idea to keep your tiles hidden when playing dominoes?
7. What if you can't find the Frisbee you threw?
8. What does a good sport do when he loses?
9. What does a good sport do when he wins?
10. How do you and a friend decide what you want to do together?

Gym

Receptive Vocabulary
Name each picture the client points to.

1. Point to the treadmill (locker room, stationary bike, weight machine, step machine, free weights).
2. Where do you change clothes?
3. Which do you ride?
4. Which do you run on?
5. Which is like climbing stairs?
6. Which do you lift?
7. Which make your heart pump faster?
8. Which build muscles?
9. Which are at a gym?
10. Which have you tried?

Receptive Activities
Before doing these activities, make two copies of the picture grid. Cut apart one grid to make picture cards.

1. Give the client the picture grid. Have him match the picture cards to the pictures on the grid. *Where is/are the _____?*
2. Play a game of Bingo. Use pennies as markers.
3. Cover three to six pictures on the picture grid. Show the client a picture card and have him tell you where it was on the picture grid. *Where was the _____?*
4. Place the picture cards faceup on the table. Have the client follow your directions. *Touch the _____. Take the _____. Hand me the _____. Point to the _____. Turn over the _____.*
5. Use ads from a sporting goods store or find a website that includes workout equipment by typing "exercise equipment" on an Internet search engine. *Find (a/an) _____.*
6. Visit the weight room at your school. Find these items and have the client do some exercises. *Find (a) _____.*
7. Visit a sporting goods store or tour a gym. Give the client the picture cards. *Let's look for (a) _____.*

Word/Sentence Imitation and Sentence Completion
1. Ask the client to repeat each word after you say it. *Say _____.*
2. Use each word to complete the sentence *Let's go to the _____.* Have the client repeat your sentences.
3. Print *He uses the _____* on a card. Have the client complete the sentence using the vocabulary words.

Expressive Vocabulary
1. Name each picture.
2. What do all of these items have in common?
3. What do you do in a locker room?
4. How do you use a treadmill?
5. What do you do on a stationary bike?
6. How do you use a step machine?
7. What do you do with free weights?
8. How do you use a weight machine?
9. Name two places you can find exercise equipment.
10. (Cover the pictures.) Name five pieces of exercise equipment.

Expressive Activity
Help the client make an exercise plan. Have the client talk about which exercises increase muscle strength and which increase aerobic ability. Let him write down which exercises to do, how often to do them, and how long or how many repetitions to do.

Critical Thinking and Problem Solving
1. If you want to build muscles, what exercises could you do?
2. If you want to run faster, what exercises could you do?
3. Which exercises make your heart beat faster?
4. How is this good for your heart?
5. If you want to lose weight, what could you do?
6. How does what you eat affect your health?
7. What are some benefits to exercising?
8. How could you convince a friend to exercise more?
9. If you want to go to a gym, how could you invite a friend?
10. What exercise goals do you have?

Vocabulary During Leisure Activities: Horseback Riding

Horseback Riding

Receptive Vocabulary
Name each picture the client points to.

1. Point to the ramp (saddle, reins, horse, stirrups, helmet).
2. Which do you sit on?
3. Where do you put your feet?
4. Which protects your head?
5. Which do you hold in your hands?
6. Which is sloped?
7. Which is an animal?
8. Which steer the horse?
9. Which go on a horse?
10. Which have you seen?

Receptive Activities
Before doing these activities, make two copies of the picture grid. Cut apart one grid to make picture cards.

1. Give the client the picture grid. Have her match the picture cards to the pictures on the grid. *Where is/are the _____?*
2. Play a game of Bingo. Use pennies as markers.
3. Cover three to six pictures on the picture grid. Show the client a picture card and have her tell you where it was on the picture grid. *Where was/were the _____?*
4. Look for pictures of the vocabulary words by typing "therapeutic riding" on the images feature of an Internet search engine. *Find (a) _____.*
5. Role-play riding a horse. Use a real helmet or a cap to pretend. Use a blanket for the saddle, and a jumprope for the reins. Use a bench, rolled up mat, or straddle a chair for the horse. Use the vocabulary words to give the client directions to follow throughout the activity. *Put on a helmet. Put the saddle on the horse. Sit on the horse. Hold the reins.*
6. Visit a therapeutic riding center. Let the clients tour or ride the horses. *Let's look for (a) _____.*

Word/Sentence Imitation and Sentence Completion
1. Ask the client to repeat each word after you say it. *Say _____.*
2. Use each word to complete the sentence *I use (a) _____.* Have the client repeat your sentences.
3. Print *I see (a) _____* on a card. Have the client complete the sentence using the vocabulary words.

Expressive Vocabulary
1. Name each picture.
2. What do all of these items have in common?
3. What does a helmet do?
4. How do we use a ramp?
5. Describe a horse.
6. What do we do with a saddle?
7. What do we do with stirrups?
8. What do we do with reins?
9. Describe how you'd get on a horse.
10. (Cover the pictures.) Name six items you'd see at a horseback riding center.

Expressive Activity
Let the client role-play planning a trip to a therapeutic riding center. Have her find out which days and hours the center is open, how much it costs, and make a reservation. She can also plan who will go to the center, how they'll get there, how much money each person should bring, and how to get permission for everyone to go.

Critical Thinking and Problem Solving
1. How could you plan a trip to a horseback riding center?
2. What if you have trouble fastening the helmet?
3. What if you need help mounting the horse?
4. What if you are afraid to mount a horse?
5. What could you ask if you don't know how to ride a horse?
6. What if your horse gets too close to the horse in front of you?
7. What are some things you might see while riding a horse?
8. How do you think it would feel to ride on a horse?
9. How do people take good care of horses?
10. Would you like to ride a horse? Why?

Vocabulary During Leisure Activities: Miniature Golf

Miniature Golf

Receptive Vocabulary
Name each picture the client points to.

1. Point to the golf ball (golf club, score card).
2. Point to putt (par, hole in one).
3. Which do you hit the ball with?
4. Which is round and bumpy?
5. Which is the target score for a hole?
6. Which do you write the score on?
7. Which means "to hit the ball lightly"?
8. Which means "to hit the ball in the hole in one try"?
9. Which would you see at a golf course?
10. Which would you see at a miniature golf course?

Receptive Activities
Before doing these activities, make two copies of the picture grid. Cut apart one grid to make picture cards.

1. Give the client the picture grid. Have him match the picture cards to the pictures on the grid. *Where is the _____?*
2. Play a game of Bingo. Use pennies as markers.
3. Bring in a real golf ball and a golf club. Let the clients play a small game of golf in your room. They can putt golf balls into a box set on its side. You can increase the challenge by adding obstacles, such as cones, mats, or wedges. Using the vocabulary words, give the clients directions to follow throughout the activity. *Putt the golf ball. Mark a 3 on your score card. Try to get a hole in one.*
4. Place the picture cards faceup on the table. Have the client follow your directions. *Touch (the) _____. Take (the) _____. Hand me (the) _____. Point to (the) _____. Turn over (the) _____.*
5. Cover three to six pictures on the picture grid. Show the client a picture card and have him tell you where it was on the picture grid. *Where was the _____?*
6. Visit a miniature golf course or driving range. Use the vocabulary while playing. *It's your turn to putt. What's par for this hole? Here's your golf ball.*

Word/Sentence Imitation and Sentence Completion
1. Ask the client to repeat each word after you say it. *Say _____.*
2. Use each word to complete the sentence *I'd like a _____.* Have the client repeat your sentences.
3. Print *This is (a) _____* on a card. Have the client complete the sentence using the vocabulary words.

Expressive Vocabulary
1. Name each picture.
2. What do all of these things have in common?
3. What do you do with a golf club?
4. Describe a golf ball.
5. What do you do with a score card?
6. Tell how to putt the ball.
7. What is a hole in one?
8. What does "par" mean?
9. Describe how to play miniature golf.
10. (Cover the pictures.) Name six golf terms.

Expressive Activity
Let the client role-play planning a trip to a miniature golf course. Have him plan who will go, how they'll get there, how much money each person should bring, and getting permission.

Critical Thinking and Problem Solving
1. How could you make a plan to visit a miniature golf course with a friend?
2. What do you need to consider when planning the activity?
3. Why is it a good idea to look at the layout of the hole before teeing off?
4. After each person has teed off, who goes next?
5. What do you do if your golf ball is too close to the curb?
6. What do you do if your golf ball goes into the water?
7. What strategies do you use at a hole with a spinning windmill?
8. What strategies do you use at a hole with an anthill?
9. What does a good sport do when he or she is losing? winning?
10. Do you like miniature golf? Why?

Vocabulary During Leisure Activities: Movie Theater

Movie Theater

Receptive Vocabulary
Name each picture the client points to.

1. Point to the theater (marquee, preview, cashier, concession stand, ticket).
2. Which lists the movies?
3. Which shows clips from upcoming movies?
4. Where do you sit?
5. Who do you pay?
6. Which paper shows you paid?
7. Where do you buy snacks?
8. Which is outside in front of a movie theater?
9. Which are inside a movie theater?
10. Which have you seen?

Receptive Activities
Before doing these activities, make two copies of the picture grid. Cut apart one grid to make picture cards.

1. Give the client the picture grid. Have her match the picture cards to the pictures on the grid. *Where is the _____?*
2. Play a game of Bingo. Use pennies as markers.
3. Role-play going to a movie theater. Practice looking at the movie choices and times, paying the cashier, buying popcorn (microwaved in class), and watching a movie (a video or DVD).
4. Place the picture cards faceup on the table. Have the client follow your directions. *Touch the _____. Take the _____. Hand me the _____. Point to the _____. Turn over the _____.*
5. Look through the entertainment section of a newspaper or on the Internet on a movie theater website. Find movies of interest. *Look for a movie theater.*
6. Visit a movie theater. Find the people or items that match the picture cards. *Let's look for a _____.*

Word/Sentence Imitation and Sentence Completion
1. Ask the client to repeat each word after you say it. *Say _____.*
2. Use each word to complete the sentence *I see the _____.* Have the client repeat your sentences.
3. Print *This is a _____* on a card. Have the client complete the sentence using the vocabulary words.

Expressive Vocabulary
1. Name each picture.
2. What do all of these items and people have in common?
3. What is on a marquee?
4. What does a cashier do?
5. What do you do with a ticket?
6. Name three things sold at a concession stand.
7. Describe what a theater looks like inside.
8. What is a preview for?
9. What kinds of movies do you like?
10. (Cover the pictures.) Name six people or items you'd see at a movie theater.

Expressive Activity
Have the clients role-play going to a movie theater. Let them take turns being the cashier at the ticket counter, selling concessions, purchasing tickets and snacks. Then show a video or DVD. Have the clients use the vocabulary words throughout the activity to talk about what's going on.

Critical Thinking and Problem Solving
1. How can you find out what movies are playing in your area?
2. How can you find out when and where the movies are playing?
3. How could you make a plan to see a movie with a friend?
4. What could you and a friend talk about to decide which movie to see?
5. What if you and your friend like different movies?
6. Why is it a good idea to discuss the day, time, transportation, and permission before going to the movies with a friend?
7. What if you planned to see one movie, but when you got to the theater, it was sold out?
8. What if you want to buy a large popcorn, but you don't have enough money?
9. Why is it a good idea to sit quietly during a movie?
10. What could you say to your friend if you had a good time with her at the movie?

Poker

Receptive Vocabulary
Name each picture the client points to.

1. Point to one pair (three of a kind, full house, two pairs, straight, flush)
2. Which hand has one match?
3. Which hand has two matches?
4. Which has all hearts?
5. What has numbers in order?
6. Which has three cards that match?
7. Which has a pair and three of a kind?
8. Which are poker hands?
9. Which hand is the highest?
10. Which hand is the lowest?

Receptive Activities
Before doing these activities, make two copies of the picture grid. Cut apart one grid to make picture cards.

1. Give the client the picture grid. Have him match the picture cards to the pictures on the grid. *Where is the _____?*
2. Play a game of Bingo. Use pennies as markers.
3. Give the client a copy of the picture grid. Place five playing cards faceup on the table so that they show one of the vocabulary words (e.g., full house). Have the client point to the picture that matches the hand. *Find (the) _____.*
4. Sequence the picture cards in order from the lowest hand to the highest hand. *The best hand here is the flush. Show me the flush. (Give similar directions for the other hands.)*
5. Scramble the picture cards and ask the client to put them in order. *Put these hands in order from the lowest to the highest. (Name each hand the client correctly places in order.)*
6. Play a game of poker—Texas Hold'em or Five Card Draw. While the clients are learning the game, they can all show their cards so you can guide them. Use the vocabulary words while giving them instructions.

Word/Sentence Imitation and Sentence Completion
1. Ask the client to repeat each word after you say it. *Say _____.*
2. Use each word to complete the sentence *He has (a) _____.* Have the client repeat your sentences.
3. Print *I see (a) _____* on a card. Have the client complete the sentence using the vocabulary words.

Expressive Vocabulary
1. Name each picture.
2. What do all of these pictures have in common?
3. Describe three different pairs you could get.
4. Tell what "three of a kind" means.
5. Explain what a "straight" is.
6. Describe what "flush" means.
7. Tell what a "full house" is.
8. What is the highest pair you could get?
9. What is the highest hand you could get?
10. (Cover the pictures.) Name six different poker hands.

Expressive Activity
Let the clients play poker. Have them use the vocabulary words to name what they have in their hands at the end of each round.

Critical Thinking and Problem Solving
1. How would you ask some friends to play poker with you?
2. If two people get a pair, how do you decide which pair is higher?
3. If two people get the same pair, how do you decide which hand is higher?
4. If two people get three of a kind, how do you decide which hand is higher?
5. If two people get a straight, how do you decide which hand is higher?
6. Why is it a good idea to pay attention to when it is your turn?
7. When you are dealt your cards, how do you decide whether to stay in or fold?
8. What does a good sport do when he's losing?
9. What does a good sport do when he's winning?
10. Do you like to play poker? Why?

Soccer

Receptive Vocabulary
Name each picture the client points to.

1. Point to the soccer ball (cleats, shin guards, goal, dribble, throw-in).
2. Which go on your feet?
3. Which go on your legs?
4. Which do you kick?
5. Where do you want the ball to go?
6. Who is tossing the ball into the game?
7. Who is kicking the ball?
8. Which items are used in a soccer game?
9. Which are soccer actions?
10. Which have you done?

Receptive Activities
Before doing these activities, make two copies of the picture grid. Cut apart one grid to make picture cards.

1. Give the client the picture grid. Have her match the picture cards to the pictures on the grid. *Where is/are (the) _____?*
2. Play a game of Bingo. Use pennies as markers.
3. Cover three to six pictures on the picture grid. Show the client a picture card and have her tell you where it was on the picture grid. *Where was/were (the) _____?*
4. Use ads from a sporting goods store or a discount department store. *Find (a/an) _____.*
5. Let the clients practice playing soccer. It can be a real game outside on a soccer field or a modified game with a beach ball. Have the clients take turns dribbling, throwing-in, and kicking a soccer ball into a goal. Use the vocabulary words to give the clients directions to follow throughout the activity. *It's your turn to dribble the ball. You scored a goal!*
6. Visit a sporting goods store or a discount department store. Use the pictures as a shopping list. *Let's look for (a) _____.*

Word/Sentence Imitation and Sentence Completion
1. Ask the client to repeat each word after you say it. *Say _____.*
2. Use each word to complete the sentence *This is a/These are _____.* Have the client repeat your sentences.
3. Print *I see (a) _____* on a card. Have the client complete the sentence using the vocabulary words.

Expressive Vocabulary
1. Name each picture.
2. What do all of these pictures have in common?
3. How do you put on shin guards?
4. Describe a soccer ball.
5. How are cleats different from other shoes?
6. Describe a soccer goal.
7. Explain how to do a throw-in.
8. Tell how to dribble a soccer ball.
9. Where can you play soccer?
10. (Cover the pictures.) Name six soccer words.

Expressive Activity
Let the client role-play organizing a soccer game. Have her discuss who will be on the teams, where they'll play the game, and what equipment they'll need. Encourage her to use the vocabulary words throughout the activity.

Critical Thinking and Problem Solving
1. What do you need to consider when planning a soccer game?
2. Why is it a good idea to wear shin guards when playing soccer?
3. Why is it a good idea to wear cleats?
4. How does a team win a soccer game?
5. How do you know which way to run with the ball?
6. Why is it a good idea to talk with your teammates?
7. What happens if you touch the ball with your hands?
8. What does a good sport do when her team is losing?
9. What does a good sport do when her team is winning?
10. Do you like soccer? Why?